ZAGATSURVEY®

2007

BEST OF
NEW ORLEANS

- Restaurants
- Nightlife
- Attractions
- Hotels

**Local Editors: Sharon Litwin,
Mimi Read and Todd A. Price**

Staff Editor: Karen Hudes

Published and distributed by
ZAGAT SURVEY, LLC
4 Columbus Circle
New York, New York 10019
Tel: 212 977 6000
E-mail: neworleans@zagat.com
Web site: www.zagat.com

Acknowledgments

We thank John Abajian, Patricia Chandler, Pat Denechaud, William A. Fagaly, Charlotte Norman, Andrea Mahady Price, Alex Rawls, Steven Shukow, Scott Simmons, Jacqueline Sullivan, Katie Walenter, as well as the following members of our staff: Victoria Elmacioglu (assistant editor), Sean Beachell, Maryanne Bertollo, Reni Chin, Larry Cohn, Bill Corsello, David Downing, Andrew Eng, Jeff Freier, Michelle Golden, Roy Jacob, Natalie Lebert, Mike Liao, Dave Makulec, Andre Pilette, Becky Ruthenberg, Troy Segal, Thomas Sheehan, Kilolo Strobert, Sharon Yates and Kyle Zolner.

All those who came to New Orleans in the earliest post-Katrina days – first responders, returning evacuees, volunteers and the National Guard – will never forget the numerous chefs and restaurateurs who found ways to cook for those who needed to be fed. There were so many it's impossible to recognize them all here, but Tommy Cvitanovich of Metairie's Drago's, Paul Prudhomme of K-Paul's and Scott Boswell of Stella! (both in the French Quarter) stand out for their devotion and generosity.

This book is dedicated to Austin Leslie, Joseph Casamento and Mary and Ernest Hansen, who each contributed so much to New Orleans' culinary culture. All died shortly after Katrina.

Contents

About This Survey

Here are the results of our *2007 Best of New Orleans Survey*, covering 513 restaurants, bars and attractions as tested by 3,637 surveyors. We've also included a selection of leading hotels as rated by avid travelers. To help you navigate New Orleans' dining scene, we have prepared a number of lists. See Most Popular and Key Newcomers (page 9), Top Ratings (pages 10–15) and Best Buys (page 16). Nightlife lists begin on page 113; for top Attractions and Hotels, see pages 140 and 149. In addition, we have provided 70 handy indexes.

This marks the 28th year that Zagat Survey has reported on the shared experiences of people like you. What started in 1979 as a hobby involving 200 of our friends rating NYC restaurants has come a long way. Today we have over 250,000 active surveyors and now cover dining, entertaining, golf, hotels, movies, music, nightlife, resorts, shopping, spas, theater and tourist attractions around the world. All of these guides are based on consumer surveys. They are also available by subscription at zagat.com, and for use on BlackBerry, Palm, Windows Mobile devices and mobile phones.

By regularly surveying large numbers of avid customers, we hope to have achieved a uniquely current and reliable series of guides. In effect, these guides are the restaurant industry's report card, since each place's ratings and review are really a free market study of its own customers.

Of 3,600-plus surveyors who participated this year, 48% are women, 52% men; the breakdown by age is 12% in their 20s; 24%, 30s; 23%, 40s; 26%, 50s; and 15%, 60s or above. Our editors have done their best to synopsize these surveyors' opinions, with their direct comments shown in quotation marks. We sincerely thank each of these people; this book is really "theirs."

We are especially grateful to our editors, Sharon Litwin, the senior vice president of the Louisiana Philharmonic Orchestra and founding president of the Crescent City Farmers Market; Mimi Read, who writes about food, architecture and design for national magazines; and Todd A. Price, food editor at *OffBeat* magazine and a contributor to other publications.

Finally, we invite you to join any of our upcoming *Surveys*. To do so, just register at zagat.com, where you can rate and review any restaurant, nightspot, hotel or attraction at any time during the year. Each participant will receive a free copy of the resulting guide when it is published. Your comments and even criticisms of this guide are also solicited. There is always room for improvement with your help. You can contact us at neworleans@zagat.com.

New York, NY
January 3, 2007

Nina and Tim

Nina and Tim Zagat

What's New

The heartening, maybe even amazing, thing about New Orleans is that there still is a New Orleans, deeply wounded, to be sure, but still kickin' and filled with extraordinary people who are rebuilding this most historic city. Already the core of our dining scene is back – more than 360 of the 565 restaurants last featured by Zagat have reopened, and 83% of surveyors are eating out as much as or more than they did before Katrina.

Good Times Are Rolling: The French Quarter and most of Uptown ("the sliver by the river"), both of which dodged the flood, have bounced back in style. While we mourn the loss of culinary jewels Bella Luna, Bistro at Maison de Ville, Cobalt, Louis XVI, Mandich and Sid-Mar, to name a few, we're thrilled that Commander's Palace has returned, more beautiful than ever. Among the city's shining stars, John Besh's August continues to delight the most demanding gourmets, Galatoire's is still packed for long, leisurely lunches and New Orleans Grill is sizzling once again. For a nightcap, Maple Leaf remains tops for big bands, and the new Chickie Wah Wah and Jin Jean's are shaking up the music scene.

It's a Brave New World: A number of post-Katrina openings defied the odds, chief among them Vizard's on the Avenue by veteran chef Kevin Vizard, the Cajun-reviving Cochon by Donald Link and buzzing Alberta's by up-and-comer Melody Pate. Hot on their heels, Todd English opened the brasserie Riche as his first venture in the Crescent City.

And It's Not Over Yet: Raring for a comeback in early 2007 are Barreca's, Blue Plate Cafe, Gabrielle and Steak Knife, as well as the big fat burgers at Lakeview Harbor and oyster po' boys at Mandina's. The equally beloved Dooky Chase and Mr. B's are also on deck. See zagat.com for updates.

Challenges Ahead: While travelers who stick to time-honored tourist sites might be lulled into thinking the whole city's back on its feet – aside from staffing shortages at restaurants and other businesses – the truth remains that much of New Orleans is still uninhabitable and many working-class people have not been able to return. To view the hardest hit areas and learn what the city is doing to move forward, visitors can take one of several educational bus tours; see page 140 for more information.

Keeping Tabs: Even with all the hardships of the past 16 months, New Orleanians' love of eating out together has provided sustenance and comfort, and we can still dine superbly on an affordable average price per meal of $26 – well below the national mean. So come on down and join us – we promise you'll pass a good time!

New Orleans, LA
January 3, 2007

Sharon Litwin

Ratings & Symbols

Name, Address, Phone Number & Web Site

Zagat Ratings

Hours & Credit Cards

F	D	S	C
▽ 23	9	13	$15

Tim & Nina's ◐ ☒ ⊄

6400 Tchoupitoulas St. (Laurel St.), 504-555-3867; www.zagat.com

"It's definitely no croc" at this "gargantuan gator house" that "fries, sautés and flambés" its "trendy" specialty into "more than just a swamp thing"; though respondents "wrestle with loving the place" – the decor looks "dredged from the bayou" and service "could be snappier" – the cooking's so "sharp" that boatloads of locals can't stop biting at its Garden District door.

Review, with surveyors' comments in quotes

Top Spots: Places with the highest overall ratings, popularity and importance are listed in BLOCK CAPITAL LETTERS.

Hours: ◐ serves after 11 PM
☒ closed on Sunday
Ⓜ closed on Monday

Credit Cards: ⊄ no credit cards accepted

Ratings are on a scale of **0** to **30**.

F	Food	D	Decor	S	Service	C	Cost
23		9		13		$15	

0–9 poor to fair	**20–25** very good to excellent
10–15 fair to good	**26–30** extraordinary to perfection
16–19 good to very good	▽ low response/less reliable

Cost (C): Reflects our surveyors' average estimate of the price of a dinner with one drink and tip and is a benchmark only. Lunch is usually 25% less.

For newcomers or survey write-ins listed without ratings, the price range is indicated as follows:

I	$25 and below	**E**	$41 to $65
M	$26 to $40	**VE**	$66 or more

Most Popular Places

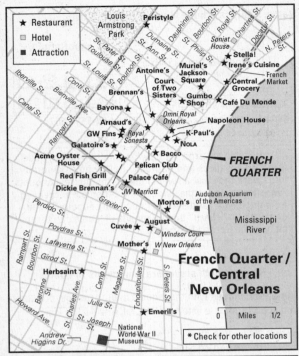

French Quarter / Central New Orleans

Legend:
★ Restaurant
▢ Hotel
■ Attraction

Louis Armstrong Park
Peristyle
Soniat House
Stella!
Antoine's
Muriel's
Jackson Square
Irene's Cuisine
Brennan's
Court of Two Sisters
Central Grocery
French Market
Gumbo Shop
Café Du Monde
Bayona
Omni Royal Orleans
Arnaud's
Napoleon House
GW Fins
Royal Sonesta
K-Paul's
Galatoire's
NoLa
Acme Oyster House
Bacco
FRENCH QUARTER
Pelican Club
Red Fish Grill
Palace Café
Dickie Brennan's
JW Marriott
Morton's
Audubon Aquarium of the Americas
Mississippi River
August
Cuvée
Windsor Court
W New Orleans
Mother's
Herbsaint
Emeril's
National World War II Museum

0 Miles 1/2

* Check for other locations

New Orleans

Lake Pontchartrain
Robert E. Lee Blvd.
Drago's
Veterans Memorial Blvd.
West End Blvd.
Elysian Fields Ave.
Ruth's Chris
Acme Oyster House
Canal Blvd.
City Park
Florida Ave.
Metairie
Causeway Blvd.
Airline Hwy.
Esplanade Ave.
Carrollton Ave.
Canal Ave.
Tulane Ave.
Pontchartrain Expy.
Detail above
Jacques-Imo's Cafe
Brigtsen's
St. Charles Ave.
Jefferson Ave.
Napoleon Ave.
Louisiana Ave.
Jackson Ave.
Zea*
Audubon Park
La Crêpe Nanou
Upperline
Lilette
Audubon Zoo
Magazine Ave.
Tchoupitoulas St.
Clancy's
Dick & Jenny's
La Petite Grocery
Mississippi River

Miles
0   1

8   subscribe to zagat.com

Most Popular Places

Each surveyor has been asked to name his or her five favorite restaurants. This list reflects their choices.

1. Galatoire's	21. Bacco
2. Bayona	22. Herbsaint
3. Café Du Monde	23. Cuvée
4. NOLA	24. Red Fish Grill*
5. Emeril's	25. GW Fins
6. Brennan's	26. Stella!
7. Acme Oyster	27. La Crêpe Nanou
8. K-Paul's	28. Palace Café
9. August	29. Central Grocery
10. Antoine's	30. Drago's
11. Brigtsen's	31. Irene's Cuisine
12. Jacques-Imo's	32. Lilette
13. Clancy's	33. Gumbo Shop
14. Upperline	34. Muriel's Jackson Sq.
15. Mother's	35. Morton's
16. Arnaud's	36. La Petite Grocery
17. Dick & Jenny's	37. Ruth's Chris
18. Dickie Brennan's	38. Napoleon House
19. Court of Two Sisters	39. Pelican Club
20. Peristyle	40. Zea

Our Most Popular list wouldn't be complete without mention of **Commander's Palace,** which earned the No. 1 spot for 17 years in a row, pre-Katrina. It reopened on October 1, 2006, following the completion of this year's survey. However, by all reports it is once again playing at the top of its game. If popularity were calibrated to price, many other restaurants would join the above ranks. Therefore we've added a list of 80 Best Buys on Page 16. Finally, the map on page 8 includes the Most Popular restaurants and attractions as well as several top hotels. For Most Popular nightspots, see page 113.

Key Newcomers
For a full list of Newcomers, see page 102.

Alberta	La Boca
Anatole	Riche
Cochon	7 on Fulton
Iris	Vizard's on the Ave.

* Indicates a tie with restaurant above

Top Restaurant Ratings

Excluding places with low voting.

Food

28 August
Brigtsen's
Bayona
Stella!
Alberta
Cuvée
27 La Provence
Mosca's
Vizard's on the Ave.*
Jacques-Imo's
Clancy's
Dakota, The
Galatoire's
K-Paul's
Herbsaint
Dick & Jenny's
26 Upperline
Dickie Brennan's
Irene's Cuisine
Lilette

Sal & Judy's
Shogun
Pelican Club
Le Parvenu
NOLA
La Petite Grocery
Arnaud's
Peristyle
Crabby Jack's
Lola's
25 Drago's
Domilise's
Emeril's
Iris
Joint, The
Royal China
GW Fins
Kim Son
Casamento's
Tommy's Cuisine

By Cuisine

American (New)
28 Bayona
Stella!
27 Herbsaint
26 Pelican Club
Le Parvenu

American (Traditional)
24 Port of Call
Mother's
23 Parasol's
22 Feelings Cafe
Surrey's Juice Bar

Barbecue
25 Joint, The
24 Hillbilly BBQ
19 Corky's BBQ
Ugly Dog Saloon
17 Bywater BBQ

Cajun
27 K-Paul's
25 Cochon
New Orleans Food
24 Bon Ton Café
Rest. des Familles

Chinese
25 Royal China
24 Trey Yuen
22 Café East
Five Happiness
P.F. Chang's

Coffeehouses
24 Morning Call
Café Du Monde
22 Caffe! Caffe!
19 PJ's Coffee
CC's Coffee

Coffee Shops/Diners
23 Coffee Rani
22 Elizabeth's
20 Bluebird Cafe
19 Russell's Marina
18 Clover Grill

Contemporary Louisiana
28 Brigtsen's
27 Dakota, The
26 Upperline
NOLA
25 Emeril's

Creole
28 Cuvée
27 Vizard's on the Ave.
Jacques-Imo's
Clancy's
Galatoire's

Dessert
29 Hansen's Sno-Bliz
25 Croissant d'Or
24 La Crêpe Nanou
20 La Madeleine
19 Coffee Cottage

French
28 August
27 La Provence
26 Peristyle
24 Broussard's
Dominique's

French (Bistro)
28 Alberta
26 Lilette
La Petite Grocery
25 Martinique Bistro
Etoile

Hamburgers
24 Port of Call
21 Lee's Hamburgers
18 Clover Grill
17 New Orleans Hamburger
GB's Patio B&G

Italian
27 Mosca's
26 Irene's Cuisine
Sal & Judy's
25 Tommy's Cuisine
24 Impastato's

Japanese
26 Shogun
24 Horinoya
Rock-n-Sake
23 NINJA
Sake Cafe

Mediterranean
22 Vega Tapas
Jamila's Cafe
Maple St. Cafe
20 Angeli on Decatur
19 Fellini's

Mexican
22 Taqueria Corona
Juan's Flying Burrito
21 Casa Garcia
20 Carreta's Grill
19 Superior Grill

Pizza
23 Theo's
R & O's
Slice
22 Mark Twain's Pizza
21 New York Pizza

Po' Boys
26 Crabby Jack's
25 Domilise's
Parkway Bakery
24 Galley
23 Parasol's

Sandwiches
24 Central Grocery
23 DiMartino's
Martin Wine Cellar
Whole Foods
19 Cafe Maspero

Seafood
25 Drago's
GW Fins
Casamento's
Martinique Bistro
RioMar

Soul Food/Southern
22 Elizabeth's
21 Café Reconcile
Fiorella's Café
Praline Connection
20 Cafe Atchafalaya

Steakhouses
26 Dickie Brennan's
25 Ruth's Chris
Rib Room
24 Morton's
Besh Steak

Thai/Vietnamese
25 Kim Son
Nine Roses
Pho Tau Bay
23 La Thai
Singha

Top Food

By Special Feature

Breakfast
24 New Orleans Grill
   Petunia's
   7 on Fulton
   Mother's
22 Surrey's

Brunch
27 La Provence
26 Arnaud's
25 Brennan's
24 Ralph's on Park
   Café Degas

Business Dining
28 August
   Cuvée
27 Galatoire's
   Herbsaint
26 Dickie Brennan's

Child-Friendly
27 Mosca's
25 Domilise's
23 Coffee Rani
22 Zea
   Five Happiness

Dining Alone
26 Upperline
   Pelican Club
   NOLA
25 Cochon
23 Pascal's Manale

Family-Style
26 Shogun
25 Royal China
   Kim Son
   New Orleans Food
24 Mother's

Hotel Dining
28 Stella!
   Hôtel Provincial
27 Vizard's on the Ave.
   Garden District
25 Rib Room
   Omni Royal Orleans
24 New Orleans Grill
   Windsor Court Hotel
   Café Adelaide
   Loews New Orleans

Late Dining
24 Port of Call
22 Little Tokyo
21 Delachaise, The
   13 Monaghan
20 Angeli on Decatur

Newcomers/Rated
28 Alberta
27 Vizard's on the Ave.
25 Iris
   Cochon
24 7 on Fulton

Offbeat
27 Jacques-Imo's
   Dick & Jenny's
25 Mat & Naddie's
24 Central Grocery
   Café Degas

People-Watching
28 Bayona
27 Vizard's on the Ave.
   Clancy's
   Galatoire's
   K-Paul's

Power Scenes
28 August
27 Galatoire's
26 La Petite Grocery
   Arnaud's
   Peristyle

Quiet Conversation
28 Cuvée
27 La Provence
26 Le Parvenu
24 New Orleans Grill
   Broussard's

Trendy
28 Alberta
27 Vizard's on the Ave.
   Herbsaint
   Dick & Jenny's
26 Lilette

Winning Wine Lists
28 Brigtsen's
   Bayona
   Cuvée
27 Clancy's
26 Arnaud's

By Location

Carrollton/Riverbend
28 Brigtsen's
27 Jacques-Imo's
25 Iris
   Mat & Naddie's
24 One Restaurant

Central Business District
28 August
   Cuvée
24 New Orleans Grill
   Bon Ton Café
   Café Adelaide

Covington
27 Dakota, The
25 New Orleans Food
   Etoile
23 Coffee Rani
18 Copeland's

Faubourg Marigny
23 Bank Cafe
   Adolfo's
   Wasabi
22 Feelings Cafe
   Marigny Brasserie

French Quarter
28 Bayona
   Stella!
27 Galatoire's
   K-Paul's
26 Dickie Brennan's

Garden District
27 Vizard's on the Ave.
23 Sake Cafe
   Parasol's
   Slice
22 Zea

Gretna
25 Kim Son
   Nine Roses
   Pho Tau Bay
23 DiMartino's
   Tony Mandina's

Harahan
22 Zea
   Taqueria Corona
20 Reginelli's
   La Madeleine
19 Coffee Cottage

Kenner
26 Le Parvenu
23 Sake Cafe
   Harbor Seafood
22 Zea
19 Brick Oven Cafe

Mandeville
24 Trey Yuen
23 Coffee Rani
   Nuvolari's
22 Caffe! Caffe!
   Little Tokyo

Metairie
26 Shogun
25 Drago's
   Royal China
   Ruth's Chris
24 Morning Call

Mid-City
26 Lola's
25 Parkway Bakery
24 Liuzza's by Track
22 Popeyes
   Juan's Flying Burrito

Uptown
28 Alberta
27 Clancy's
   Dick & Jenny's
26 Upperline
   Lilette

Warehouse District
27 Herbsaint
25 Emeril's
   Tommy's Cuisine
   Cochon
   RioMar

Top Decor

28	New Orleans Grill	Peristyle
	August	Brennan's
27	Rest. des Familles	Café Adelaide
	Etoile	Court of Two Sisters
	Ralph's on Park	Antoine's
26	Cuvée	Sake Cafe
	Muriel's Jackson Sq.	Le Parvenu
	La Provence	Pelican Club
	Café East	Upperline
	Galatoire's	Emeril's
25	Bayona	Bourbon House
	Stella!	La Petite Grocery
	Arnaud's	Trey Yuen
	Broussard's	Palace Café
	Civello's	Napoleon House
	Feelings Cafe*	Vizard's on the Ave.
	Dickie Brennan's	**23** Begue's
	GW Fins	Bacco
	Rib Room	Lilette
24	La Côte Brasserie	La Crêpe Nanou

Outdoors

Bayona	Feelings Cafe
Brennan's	Iris
Broussard's	La Crêpe Nanou
Coffee Rani	Martinique Bistro
Commander's Palace	Vizard's on the Ave.

Romance

Arnaud's	Feelings Cafe
Bayona	La Provence
Broussard's	Lilette
Commander's Palace	New Orleans Grill
Cuvée	Stella!

Rooms

Antoine's	Broussard's
August	Commander's Palace
Bacco	Emeril's
Bayona	New Orleans Grill
Brennan's	Riche

Views

Anatole	Oak Alley
Audubon Park	Ralph's on Park
Cafe Pontalba	Rest. des Familles
Muriel's Jackson Sq.	Superior Grill

Top Service

27 August
Brigtsen's
Galatoire's
26 Bayona
Arnaud's
Stella!
Cuvée
La Provence
25 New Orleans Grill
Civello's
Clancy's
Dickie Brennan's
Rib Room
Emeril's
Herbsaint
Upperline
Broussard's
Vizard's on the Ave.
Dakota, The
24 Tommy's Cuisine

Brennan's
NOLA
Peristyle
K-Paul's
GW Fins
Dick & Jenny's
Alberta
Antoine's
La Petite Grocery
Jamila's Cafe
Ralph's on Park*
Café Adelaide
Ruth's Chris
Morton's
Rest. des Familles
23 Pelican Club
Begue's
Cafe Giovanni
Palace Café
Bon Ton Café

Best Buys

Top Bangs for the Buck

1. Hansen's Sno-Bliz
2. Morning Call
3. CC's Coffee
4. La Boulangerie
5. PJ's Coffee
6. Café Du Monde
7. rue de la course
8. Croissant d'Or
9. Joint, The
10. Raising Cane's
11. Parkway Bakery
12. Lee's Hamburgers
13. Café Reconcile
14. 13 Monaghan
15. Roly Poly
16. DiMartino's
17. Royal Blend
18. Central Grocery
19. Russell's Short Stop
20. Domilise's
21. Clover Grill
22. Caffe! Caffe!
23. Bluebird Cafe
24. Betsy's Pancake
25. Popeyes
26. Hillbilly BBQ
27. Whole Foods
28. Chateau Coffee
29. Slice
30. Pho Tau Bay
31. Parasol's
32. Slim Goodies
33. Surrey's Juice Bar
34. Theo's
35. Juan's Flying Burrito
36. Singha
37. Liuzza's by Track
38. Mike Serio's
39. Jazmine Café
40. Crabby Jack's

Other Good Values

Acropolis
Angelo Brocato
Apple Seed
Cafe Rani
Casa Garcia
Casamento's
Churros Café
Coffea Gallery
Coffee Cottage
Elizabeth's
Fiesta Latina
Five Happiness
Frosty's Café
Galley
GB's Patio B&G
Home Furnishings
Jamila's Cafe
Jipang
Kim Son
Kosher Cajun Deli
La Madeleine
Lebanon's Café
Li'l Dizzy's
Louisiana Pizza
Martin Wine Cellar
Mona's Cafe
Mr. Gyros
New Orleans Food
New Orleans Hamburger
Nine Roses
Oscar's
P&G
Pupuseria Macarena
Reginelli's
Russell's Marina Grill
Schiro's
Steve's Diner
Sun Ray Grill
Taqueria Corona
Trolley Stop Cafe

Restaurant Directory

Abita Brew Pub Ⓜ 20 | 19 | 21 | $20

72011 Holly St. (bet. Hwys. 36 & 59), Abita Springs, 985-892-5837; www.abita.com

A "local institution", this piney, country-style microbrewery lures suds-hounds to Abita Springs for "stellar beers" "that aren't available on the shelves"; though some find its "tasty" Creole-Eclectic menu "a little pricey" for "pub food", most praise it as a "great stop if you're in the area."

ACME OYSTER HOUSE 22 | 13 | 17 | $21

724 Iberville St. (bet. Bourbon & Royal Sts.), 504-522-5973
3000 Veterans Memorial Blvd. (N. Causeway Blvd.), 504-309-4056
www.acmeoyster.com

"Eat 'em as they shuck 'em" at this "old-school" seafood duo that's "bivalve heaven" for lovers of "huge", "succulent" "fresh oysters" and "impossible-to-beat" po' boys paired with "local beers"; the French Quarter's "red-checked tablecloth" setting draws "long lines" of both tourists and natives to dig into the "cheap eats" and have a "raucous good time", while the Metairie locale is a little lower-key.

Acropolis Ⓜ – | – | – | I

3841 Veterans Blvd. (Taft Pl.), 504-888-9046

Meze mavens marvel that this tiny, friendly and affordable Metairie Med is open again, serving traditional Greek dishes with a focus on fresh fish, rounded out with some Italian touches; housed in a strip mall, the newly painted, peach-toned space, not to mention its prix fixe dinner, is welcoming to all – except for late-leaning types, since it closes at 9 PM.

Adolfo's ⊭ 23 | 15 | 18 | $25

611 Frenchmen St. (Chartres St.), 504-948-3800

"Tiny in size, big on flavor", this "consistently good", "inexpensive" Southern Italian "with a Louisiana twist" attracts a following to its second-floor digs "high atop the party on Frenchmen Street"; with its "quirky decor, service and clientele", "the atmosphere's the real charm."

ALBERTA Ⓢ Ⓜ NEW 28 | 21 | 24 | $54

5015 Magazine St. (Robert St.), 504-891-3015

Regulars whisper "don't tell" about this year-old, unmarked Uptowner where fans are "floored" by chef Melody Pate's "intricate", "avant-garde" French bistro food; though some say it's "pricey" for the neighborhood, most are "charmed" by the "kind, ebullient staff" and "hip", "jewel-box" setting with "honey-colored" lighting that flatters "everyone" – so naturally "reservations are a must."

Alpine, The 16 | 14 | 16 | $25

620 Chartres St. (Wilkinson St.), 504-523-3005; www.thealpinebistro.com

The travel-weary enjoy "watching the people pass by" at this "pleasant", "off-the-beaten-path" French Quarter old-timer; its "basic", "reliable" Cajun-Creole food works best for a "nice courtyard brunch on weekends", but no matter how "comfortable" it is, locals are leery of "any place that needs to employ a barker on the sidewalk."

Anatole NEW   – – – E

Lafayette Hotel, 600 St. Charles Ave. (Lafayette St.), 504-274-0105; www.restaurantanatole.com

Contemporary Creole seafood and aged Chicago steaks are spotlighted at this new, upscale 186-seat bistro in the CBD, where chef-owner Raymond Toups (ex Wyndam Hotel) turns out a menu of strongly executed classics that make use of prime ingredients; formerly the home of Rasputin, the spacious, handsomely renovated crimson room overlooks St. Charles Avenue.

Andrea's   22 20 22 $40

3100 19th St. (N. Causeway Blvd.), 504-834-8583; www.andreasrestaurant.com

"Don't let the strip-mall location steer you away" advise Metairie *mangiatori* who appreciate chef Andrea Apuzzo's "fine Northern Italian" fare ("especially the seafood") that "brings a touch of the Old Country to the bayou country"; while it's "a little expensive" for what you get, the "homey" interior, "accommodating staff" and live piano on the weekends make it a "solid" suburbanite.

Angeli on Decatur ●≢   20 13 16 $16

1141 Decatur St. (bet. Governor Nicholls St. & Ursuline Ave.), 504-566-0077; www.angelipizza.com

"Fabulous pizzas", "mammoth salads" and "cheap" Mediterranean eats draw an "eclectic" "hipster" crowd for "late-night" bites, after they're done "prowling" the Quarter or Frenchmen Street; despite what some find "dreary decor" and a fairly "forgetful staff", the live jazz and "classic movies projected on the wall" buoy a scene that becomes a "show in itself after midnight."

Angelo Brocato   – – – I

214 N. Carrollton Ave. (bet. Bienville Ave. & Iberville St.), 504-486-0078; www.angelobrocatoicecream.com

Locals lined up around the block the day this Mid-City institution reopened after Katrina, celebrating the return of their favorite old-world Italian ice cream and pastry shop, with its exceptional cannoli, gourmet gelati and authentic Sicilian cookies; restored to its original turn-of-the-century style, complete with wireback chairs and lit-up arches, it's just how Orleanians remember it, making it the perfect dessert stop for nostalgic grown-ups with kids in tow.

Anselmo's ☒   22 14 19 $24

3401 N. Hullen St. (15th St.), 504-889-1212

One of the first restaurants to reopen in Metairie, this "friendly neighborhood" Southern Italian serves "fresh", "excellent" red-sauce dishes in portions "usually too large to finish"; even fans admit it's "not fancy", but the "family atmosphere" makes for "enjoyable dining."

ANTOINE'S
24 | 24 | 24 | $55

713 St. Louis St. (bet. Bourbon & Royal Sts.), 504-581-4422; www.antoines.com

"You can feel the history" in this "beautiful", circa-1840 French Quarter "landmark", a Creole "grande dame" known for "classics" like oysters Rockefeller (which was invented here and "lives up to the hype"); it's long been a "special-occasion" destination for "old New Orleans society" and a tourist "must-do", but admirers report "new energy" post-Katrina, finding service "more attentive" and the recently introduced Sunday jazz brunch "simply magical."

Apple Seed Shoppe ⊠⇄
▽ 19 | 12 | 20 | $10

201 St. Charles Ave., 2nd fl. (Common St.), 504-529-3442

"Quick, healthy" meals of "freshly made salads", sandwiches and the signature cheese soup ("a staple") satisfy patrons at this pioneering vegetarian joint in the CBD; it's strictly "no-frills", but "cheap" and convenient for a lunch break.

ARNAUD'S
26 | 25 | 26 | $50

813 Bienville St. (bet. Bourbon & Dauphine Sts.), 504-523-5433; www.arnauds.com

"Old school . . . but wow" say those dazzled by this "jewel of the Quarter", a "fabulous reminder of times that were" serving "remarkable", "traditional" Creole cuisine in an "elegant" tile-paved dining room (with the house Mardi Gras museum located upstairs); from its Sunday brunch – when the "jazz is fine and the milk punch potent" – to its "gracious" service, it remains a "quintessential", if "expensive", Crescent City "original."

Audubon Park Clubhouse Ⓜ
15 | 23 | 16 | $18

Audubon Park, 6500 Magazine St. (East Dr.), 504-212-5285; www.audoboninstitute.org

"Lunch with a view" of the golf course and "beautiful moss-draped oaks" of Audubon Park beckon the "argyle-and-seersucker crowd" to the "lovely wraparound porch" at this simple yet "gloriously" situated Uptowner; its morning-to-afternoon buffet is good for "traditional club sandwiches" among other "ok food", but the real treat is bringing the kids (it's also across from the zoo) or "sipping a cocktail" at the 19th hole.

AUGUST
28 | 28 | 27 | $58

301 Tchoupitoulas St. (Gravier St.), 504-299-9777; www.rest-august.com

"Spectacular" dishes blending "European style" with "a touch of the bayou" enchant guests at this "elegant" CBD Continental–New French, ranked No. 1 in New Orleans for

Food and Service, where chef John Besh crafts a "daring" menu showcasing pristine local ingredients; the "drop-dead gorgeous" surroundings (curving brick walls, lustrous chandeliers), a "warm", "knowledgeable" staff and presentations "so beautiful you hesitate to mess up the plate" also impress, so if the tab's "pricey", you'll be "too blissed out to notice."

August Moon ☒   14 10 16 $17
3635 Prytania St. (Louisiana Ave.), 504-899-5129;
www.augustmoonneworleans.com
"A stone's throw from Tulane", this "dependable" Chinese-Vietnamese fuels up budget-conscious students and neighboring hospital workers with lunches "enough for two meals"; opinions vary over whether the eats are "sassy" and "savory" (especially the Vietnamese) or simply "generic", but most agree the "efficient takeout" and quick delivery make "to-go the way to go."

Azul ☒ NEW   ▽ 20 15 15 $35
535 Tchoupitoulas St. (Poydras St.), 504-599-2111
An "ambitious", "well-carried-out" combination of Cuban and Asian cuisine makes for "affordable, delicious" dining at this tropical-looking newcomer in the Warehouse District; critics call the menu "not quite fused" and cite an "unconcerned" staff, but the "best mojitos outside of Havana" help keep the blues at bay.

Babylon Café   21 12 16 $15
7724 Maple St. (Adams St.), 504-314-0010
"Delicious twists on the standard hummus dishes" keep this Uptown kebab-ery "full of Tulane students and neighborhood families" who find it an "excellent", "extremely affordable" choice for a "Middle Eastern fix"; true, the "decor's shabby" and the "service is slower than FEMA", but most agree it "gets the job done" – and as a bonus, there's an attached "Laundromat next door" ("doing your laundry never tasted so good").

Bacco   23 23 23 $39
W New Orleans, 310 Chartres St. (bet. Bienville Ave. & Conti St.), 504-522-2426; www.bacco.com
"The Brennan bunch does it again" at this "quality Italian in the Quarter", whose "wonderful" homemade pastas and various "contemporary" dishes offer "a good change of pace after eating étouffée all day"; the "romantic" hotel dining room and "attentive staff" enhance the "great value", but the "10-cent martinis at lunch" steal the show.

Bangkok Thai   18 10 15 $17
513 S. Carrollton Ave. (St. Charles Ave.), 504-861-3932
"They'll make it as spicy as you want" at this Riverbend "neighborhood Thai" where the "curry rocks" and the "standard" menu is "solid" and "inexpensive"; while it has

a "community feel" courtesy of the "college crowd" and "friendly staff", its "hole-in-the-wall" setting keeps the "carry-out" orders coming.

Bank Cafe, The Ⓜ   23 | 23 | 22 | $33 |
2001 Burgundy St. (Touro St.), 504-371-5260;
www.thebankcafe.com
"In a city tough on food, this one holds its own" say locals who hope "no tourist will ever find" this "slightly out-of-the-way" Contemporary Louisiana–Mediterranean, a "hip", "splendid addition to the Marigny scene"; housed in a renovated historic bank with "soaring ceilings" and an art deco bar, it's a "stunning" space for "serious yet informal" dining, though many note the "reflective surfaces" amplify the noise.

Basil Leaf   22 | 15 | 19 | $26 |
1438 S. Carrollton Ave. (Jeannette St.), 504-862-9001
"Sitting on Carrollton's Restaurant Row", this "excellent upscale Thai" offers an "unexpected menu" of "fresh, clean cuisine" including some "inventive seafood" dishes with "great presentations"; its "neighborhood feel" also appeals, even if a few find the prices relatively "steep" ("it's a better deal for lunch").

BAYONA ⓈⓂ   28 | 25 | 26 | $53 |
430 Dauphine St. (bet. Conti & St. Louis Sts.), 504-525-4455;
www.bayona.com
Fans of the "original", "peerless" New American cuisine with "global influences" created by "masterful" celeb chef-owner Susan Spicer say it "doesn't get any better" than this French Quarter "favorite", whose Creole-cottage setting has a "gracious", slightly "formal" interior and a "lovely patio"; the prix fixe options remain "a deal", and though Katrina ruined the wine cellar, an "amazing new wine list" is in place.

Beachcorner Bar & Grill ❶   ▽ 20 | 10 | 15 | $12 |
4905 Canal St. (City Park Ave.), 504-488-7357
"Big delicious burgers", "standout sweet potato fries" and other pub food at "prices that can't be beat" beckon the peckish to this "loud" Mid-City bar at the cemetery end of Canal Street; even fans say it's "still dungeonlike despite post-Katrina renovations" – but then, it's not for "frill"-seekers (or anyone under 21) anyway.

Begue's   24 | 23 | 23 | $44 |
Royal Sonesta Hotel, 300 Bourbon St. (bet. Bienville Ave. &
Conti St.), 504-553-2278; www.beguesrestaurant.com
"Always fantastic" Creole–New French food takes center stage at this French Quarter hotel dining room during its "overflowing" Friday seafood buffet and famed Sunday brunch – "not to be missed even if you're hungover"; with a courtyard view and "friendly", "well-trained" staff, it of-

fers such comforting "New Orleans hospitality" that guests are surprised to find it's almost "never crowded."

Bennachin ▽ 21 16 15 $16
1212 Royal St. (bet. Barracks & Governor Nicholls Sts.),
504-522-1230
A "welcoming" BYO with "memorable nonalcoholic drinks", this "authentic" "mom-and-pop" West African in the "quiet part of the Quarter" is the place to go for "delicious", "simple" dishes, like jambalaya-stuffed trout, baked chicken with coconut rice and a number of vegetarian choices that "let the fresh ingredients do the talking"; the "hearty meals at low prices" make up for "slow" service.

Besh Steak House at Harrah's 24 20 22 $58
Harrah's Casino, 4 Canal St. (bet. Poydras & S. Peter's Sts.),
504-533-6111; www.harrahs.com
"High-steaks gamblers" thrill to the "excellent" "prime dry-aged beef" and "novel" seafood dishes by chef John Besh (August) at this CBDer in a casino; the "knowledgeable" staff and George Rodrigue's "blue dog paintings" also have their charms, though some cite the distracting "ding, ding, ding of the slot machines" and find the cuisine "less inspired" than August's — overall a "well-done but not rare" experience.

Betsy's Pancake House 19 8 17 $11
2542 Canal St. (N. Dorgenois St.), 504-822-0213
Sassy waitresses who "must be Flo's sisters" "plunk down big, heavy breakfasts" of "awesome" flapjacks and "omelets to die for" at this "affordable" American Mid-City "family place"; even folks who say it "ain't nothing but a greasy spoon, y'all" have to reckon — "how can you not like a pancake house that also has a full bar?"

Bluebird Cafe Ⓜ⊅ 20 13 18 $12
3625 Prytania St. (bet. Antonine & Foucher Sts.), 504-895-7166
"Grits spilling off the plate", huevos rancheros *muy ricos* and "tattooed staffers slinging the best coffee" keep folks chowing down on "cheap" diner food at this Uptown breakfast and lunch "joint"; appealing to "the alternative lifestyle set" and kids alike, it's earned the kind of "line-out-the-door" "cachet" that causes caustic cool cats to hiss "been there, done that"; N.B. closed Mondays and Tuesdays.

Bon Ton Café ⊠⊅ 24 19 23 $31
401 Magazine St. (bet. Natchez & Poydras Sts.), 504-524-3386
Generations believe this CBDer is a "great example" of "old-fashioned" Cajun cuisine in a "time-warp", "traditional" place that "never got famous" — perhaps due to its "unassuming decor and casual style"; its "rich" crawfish dishes, soft-shell crab and "must-have" bread pudding, served up by "super-friendly", "chatty" waitresses, attract

the "financial district suits" for a "civilized" lunch, and a "cult following of locals" for dinner; N.B. closed weekends.

Bourbon House Seafood & Oyster Bar

| 21 | 24 | 21 | $40 |

Astor Crowne Plaza Hotel, 144 Bourbon St. (bet. Canal & Iberville Sts.), 504-522-0111; www.bourbonhouse.com
For "oysters and beer at the bar" or "well-prepared" "Gulf seafood" feasts in the "posh" dining room, Dickie Brennan's "loud", "busy" shell-shucker in the Quarter "rarely disappoints"; its "swift service" and "entertaining" view onto Bourbon Street provide additional perks for the "touristy" clientele.

Bozo's ☒ Ⓜ

| 22 | 11 | 18 | $21 |

3117 21st St. (bet. N. Causeway Blvd. & Ridgelake Dr.), 504-831-8666
"If oysters and fried seafood are your thing", Metairie fin fans say "don't miss this one" for "traditional catfish dishes" and "great po' boys" in a "nothing-fancy", "family-style" environment; just "come hungry" and "remember your map", since it's seriously "off the beaten path."

Bravo! Cucina Italia

| 19 | 20 | 18 | $24 |

Lakeside Shopping Ctr., 3413 Veterans Memorial Blvd. (Severn Ave.), 504-828-8828; www.bestitalianusa.com
"Reliable", "reasonably priced" Italian fare pulls suburbanites to this Metairie chain locale that's "definitely a step up from the Olive Garden" but "may not suffice if you're craving the authentic eats of Italia"; it's child-friendly, with the resulting "noisy atmosphere" to match, but at least the loudness is tempered by "quick" service.

BRENNAN'S

| 25 | 24 | 24 | $51 |

417 Royal St. (bet. Conti & St. Louis Sts.), 504-525-9711; www.brennansneworleans.com
"One of those places that defines old New Orleans", this Creole originator of "addictive bananas Foster" invites a "touristy" French Quarter crowd to "linger" over its famous, "decadent" "three-hour breakfast", which costs big bucks "if you do it right"; "first-rate" dinners, "Southern hospitality", a "pleasant" if "dated" dining room and a "beautiful courtyard" are pluses, and if opponents opine it's "overrated", more concur "you gotta go" "at least once."

Brick Oven Cafe Ⓜ

| 19 | 17 | 18 | $24 |

2805 Williams Blvd. (Veterans Memorial Blvd.), 504-466-2097
This "decent" Italian in Kenner serves a full menu of "classic" dishes in addition to wood-fired pizza in a "chain"-like atmosphere; its "kitschy" decor smacks of "1980s Las Vegas meets suburbia" — but regulars on their way to or from Louis Armstrong Airport "wouldn't have it any other way."

BRIGTSEN'S Ⓢ Ⓜ 28 | 22 | 27 | $47

723 Dante St. (Maple St.), 504-861-7610; www.brigtsens.com
"Genius" chef Frank Brigtsen and his "exquisite", "imaginative interpretation" of "Louisiana home cooking" provide a "true NOLA experience" at this "charming Creole cottage" in Riverbend; the blue-ribbon wine list, lively people-watching and a staff that "treats you like family" while displaying "excellent attention to detail" round out a meal that's more than "worth the cab ride"; N.B. book early.

Brothers Sushi – | – | – | M

1612 St. Charles Ave. (bet. Euterpe & Terpsichore Sts.), 504-581-4449
The three hard-working Vietnamese brothers (and one sister) who recently bought the former Tokyo Bistro have changed the name of this Garden District Japanese, but preserved the menu of fresh, generous and well-made sushi, along with distinctive soups, salads and stir-fries; details like traditional silk robes on the waiters and colorful paper lanterns add ambiance, and so do the sweeping views of St. Charles Avenue.

Broussard's 24 | 25 | 25 | $51

819 Conti St. (Bourbon St.), 504-581-3866; www.broussards.com
At this "top-notch" yet relatively "underrated" "Quarter landmark", longtime chef-owner Gunter Preuss prepares "fresh", "delicious" Creole-French fare with an "artistic" touch; the tasteful dining room and "fantastic" courtyard, combined with "high-end service" that's "old-fashioned (in a good sense)", make it a "favorite romantic spot."

Bubba Gump Shrimp Co. 12 | 15 | 14 | $25

429 Decatur St. (Conti St.), 504-522-5800; www.bubbagump.com
"If you loved the movie" you might connect to this "hokey" crustacean chain link in the Quarter, where the staff quizzes you on *Forrest Gump* trivia; otherwise, locals wonder "why oh why go here?" to eat "bland faux Louisiana seafood", suggesting that tourists "take a picture at the entrance" then "go find a real restaurant."

Bud's Broiler – | – | – | I

2008 Clearview Pkwy. (W. Napoleon Ave.), 504-889-2837●⊟
5100 Lapalco Blvd. (Barataria Blvd.), 504-348-0492 ⊟
3002 Ormond Blvd. (Plantation Rd.), 985-725-1116 ⊟
2800 Veterans Memorial Blvd. (Roosevelt Blvd.), 504-466-0026 Ⓢ
Worshiped for its charcoal-grilled hamburgers slathered with hickory-smoked sauce or chili, this local fast-food chain also whips up a mean order of chili-cheese fries and made-to-order milkshakes; such primal enticements help eaters overlook generally divey surroundings, blipping video poker machines and the grade school–sized benches and tables carved with graffiti at some locations.

Byblos
22 19 19 $24

3218 Magazine St. (bet. Harmony & Pleasant Sts.), 504-894-1233
Metarie Shopping Ctr., 1501 Metairie Rd. (bet. Bonnabel & Codifer Blvds.), 504-834-9773
2020 Veterans Memorial Blvd. (Beverly Garden Dr.), 504-837-9777

"Fresh", "amazing Middle Eastern cuisine" wins over lamb lovers at this "excellent" trio; while some call the Old Metairie branch "beautiful after renovations" and appreciate being able to get grocery store goods on Vets Highway, the Uptown locale is the most "hoppin'", particularly during the "hot" "belly dancing Thursday evening."

Bywater Bar-B-Que ⊄
17 12 15 $17

3162 Dauphine St. (Louisa St.), 504-944-4445

A "pleasant" "scruffy-artist" "eclectic atmosphere", especially at the patio bar, provides more flavor than the "passable" 'cue (some snark "basically, boiled meat drenched in BBQ sauce") at this "neighborhood" Bywater shack; but "it is what it is" shrug lackadaisical locals, who recommend you "try the daily specials" to get the best of the "cheap eats."

Café Adelaide
24 24 24 $44

Loews New Orleans Hotel, 300 Poydras St. (S. Peters St.), 504-595-3305; www.cafeadelaide.com

Owners Lally Brennan and Ti Martin, along with chef Danny Trace (Commander's Palace), preside over this "fine outpost of the Brennan empire" inside the CBD's Loews Hotel; the "Creole-inspired but not Creole-limited" menu offers "tasty", "clever re-workings of local seafood dishes", and service is generally "on its game", so even if some find the "modern" room overly "hotel lobby–like", the "New Orleans elite" is hooked.

Cafe Atchafalaya
20 16 17 $26

901 Louisiana Ave. (Laurel St.), 504-891-9626

Although followers of the longtime proprietor lament that "Iler's gone", they're relieved a "new owner" with "potential" has renovated and reopened this Garden District "shotgun house" serving "traditional Southern dishes" (including "lots of veggie choices") with "New Orleans flair"; most say the "updated look" makes for "better ambiance", even if "upscale prices" are part of the package; N.B. closed Tuesdays.

Cafe Beignet
▽ 18 13 14 $11

Musical Legends Park, 311 Bourbon St. (Bienville St.), 504-525-2611
334B Royal St. (Conti St.), 504-524-5530
www.cafebeignet.com

"This is how New Orleans does a 'fast-food' breakfast" say fans of this French Quarter Cajun duo's "quick" andouille hash browns and pastries – particularly those fried, sugar-topped beignets that demand "throwing your diet out the window"; it's a "less-crowded alternative to Café Du Monde" – and, some snipe, less special as well – but the Royal Street locale is "charming", while the Bourbon Street branch boasts a nice "outdoor area" and live weekend jazz.

Café Degas Ⓜ   24 | 22 | 21 | $32

3127 Esplanade Ave. (Ponce de Leon St.), 504-945-5635; www.cafedegas.com

Edgar himself would say "*très charmant*" to this "arty" "touch of France" on the Esplanade Ridge "down the street from NOMA"; it serves "affordable", "delectable" "classic bistro fare" on an enclosed deck reminiscent of a "tiny" "tree house" (indeed, a pecan tree grows right inside), making it a "cheery" destination whether for a "first date", Sunday brunch or "dinner with friends."

Cafe DiBlasi ⓈⓂ   20 | 16 | 20 | $24

1801-4 Stumpf Blvd. (Wright Ave.), 504-361-3106

West Bankers swear by this "family-run" Italian eatery "tucked away" in a Terrytown strip mall; with a "fresh, un-usual" menu, "friendly service" and low prices, those seeking a "neighborhood place" agree it "has it all."

CAFÉ DU MONDE ●≠   24 | 17 | 16 | $9

French Mkt., 800 Decatur St. (St. Ann St.), 504-525-4544; www.cafedumonde.com

Everyone's just gotta have the "hot", "feather-light" beig-nets ("but that's about it", foodwise) coupled with "chicory-laced coffee" at this alfresco 24/7 "institution" whose "crowded", canopied premises off Jackson Square allow for prime "people-watching" from the "wee hours" to more touristy "peak times"; sit-'n'-sippers warn of "frus-tratingly slow service" and to "be careful when you in-hale", lest you get covered with "mountains of powdered sugar" from the deep-fried "heavenly little pillows of goodness" – but that's all part of what "carries you back to antediluvian New Orleans."

CAFÉ EAST   22 | 26 | 20 | $27

4628 Rye St. (Clearview Pkwy.), 504-888-0078; www.cafeeastnola.com

"About as hip as you can be off Clearview Parkway", this "trendy", "ambitious" Metairie Chinese offers a "visual feast" of "stunning", "movie-set" decor and "elegant" food presentations; fortunately, its fusion-style "culinary delights" (some "extremely hot") also "impress", whether for a "swanky" dinner or "bang-for-the-buck" lunch.

Cafe Giovanni ⓈⓂ   23 | 22 | 23 | $40

117 Decatur St. (bet. Canal & Iberville Sts.), 504-529-2154; www.cafegiovanni.com

Music mavens appreciate a little *Tosca* with their tortellini at this French Quarter Cajun-Italian where "opera-singer waiters" "surprise and impress" from Wednesday to Saturday; most agree that chef Duke LoCicero "loves to please" and largely succeeds with his "solid", "carefully cooked" cuisine, even if it's sometimes outshined by the "wonderful entertainment."

Cafe Maspero ⊅ | 19 | 14 | 16 | $16 |
601 Decatur St. (Toulouse St.), 504-523-6250
"Huge", "hot muffalettas", "great po' boys" and other "sandwiches piled high with meat" make for "inexpensive" meals at this "touristy" French Quarter "joint" (it's "not about ambiance" here); "there's always a line", but "daiquiris for a buck" at the bar usually mollify the "mobs."

Café Pontalba | ∇ | 14 | 16 | 15 | $20 |
546 St. Peter St. (Chartres St.), 504-522-1180
"Location is everything" for this daytime French Quarter Cajun-Creole where diners gaze through "floor-length windows" onto Jackson Square; naturally, given the site, "it's a little on the touristy side", causing some locals to call the "New Orleans Disney-fied food" "ok" at best.

Cafe Rani | 20 | 18 | 18 | $19 |
2917 Magazine St. (bet. 6th & 7th Sts.), 504-895-2500
"In a city famous for fried everything, a good salad can be hard to find", but this Eclectic, "ritzy on the cheap" "lunch place" Uptown satisfies the craving with "complex combinations" of tossed greens, as well as "giant sandwiches" and "killer Bloody Marys"; grazers add, however, that "half of what makes the restaurant" is "dining under a majestic tree" in the "pleasant courtyard."

Café Reconcile ⊠⊅ | 21 | 13 | 18 | $11 |
1631 Oretha Castle Haley Blvd. (Euterpe St.), 504-568-1157; www.cafereconcile.com
"Giving back to the community" is easy as dining on "down-home Southern cooking" at this Central City "low-cost lunch option" with a "social mission" – training at-risk teens for jobs in the restaurant industry; decorated with children's artwork, the room draws everyone from "politicos to nuns" for "excellent soul food", which invites "tipping big" since "it's for a good cause"; N.B. closed evenings and weekends.

Cafe Roma | 18 | 12 | 14 | $17 |
1119 Decatur St. (bet. Governor Nicholls St. & Ursuline Ave.), 504-586-0563 ◑
Park Plaza, 3358 Paris Rd. (Josephine St.), 504-270-0999
1901 Sophie Wright Pl. (St. Mary St.), 504-524-2419 ◑
These "simple but funky" "neighborhood" pizza palaces serve "rustic" specialty pies as well as "excellent" sandwiches; their "good value", "consistency" and "prompt delivery" are part of why they're an "old favorite."

Caffe! Caffe!   22 | 17 | 19 | $14

4301 Clearview Pkwy. (W. Esplanade Ave.), 504-885-4845
3900 Hwy. 22 (Hwy. 190), Mandeville, 985-727-4222 ⓈΣ
www.caffecaffe.com

"You can smell the coffee from inside your car" as you pull up to these "neighborhood hangouts" serving "delightful salads and sandwiches" along with "great desserts" in Mandeville and Metairie; staffed by "friendly youngsters" who "manage the crowds efficiently", they're "clean and inviting" places to "meet a friend for lunch."

Calas Bistro & Wine Cellar **NEW** ▽ 25 | 26 | 21 | $33

910A W. Esplanade Ave. (Dauphine St.), 504-471-2200;
www.calasbistro.com

'Calas, hot calas!' was the cry from street vendors long ago for the "old-style Creole rice fritters" that chef Jeffrey Wagner (ex Brigtsen's) now delivers with a twist (try the "savory shrimp" version) among other "excellent" Contemporary Louisiana fare at this "bright new" Kennerite; though some say it's "still working out the kinks", the open kitchen, large windows and dark woods, plus wine flights straight from the adjoining shop, enhance what admirers agree is "just what we need at this time" — a "feel-good evening."

Cannon's   16 | 17 | 17 | $25

4141 St. Charles Ave. (Milan St.), 504-891-3200;
www.cannonsrestaurants.com

"Consistent" but "chainlike" is the consensus on this Garden District American serving "huge salads", burgers and "Creole-inspired" seafood dishes in an "open and airy" dining room; while the "lovely view of St. Charles Avenue" earns it some points, most say it's "best left to the tourists", especially during Mardi Gras.

Carmine's Italian Seafood Grill ⓂM   19 | 14 | 17 | $25

4101 Veterans Memorial Blvd. (Lake Villa Dr.), 504-455-7904
Proud paisans say "you've got to order the seafood-stuffed artichoke" at this "authentic" Metairie "family Italian" dishing up "legendary portions" of pasta covered in some of the "best red sauce outside Sicily"; the more finicky comment that "quantity over quality" results in food that's just "ok" and moan about the "slow" and "sometimes spotty service."

Carreta's Grill   20 | 15 | 18 | $17

2320 Veterans Memorial Blvd. (I-10), 504-837-6696 ⓂM
1200 W. Causeway Approach (Mandeville High Blvd.),
Mandeville, 985-727-7212
These "family-friendly", "inexpensive" Mandeville and Metairie Mexicans "soothe the cravings" for fajitas, enchiladas and more, serving "great margaritas" for the grown-ups and "fabulous cheese dip" for *muchachos*;

while the surroundings lack spice, "live mariachi music" infuses the "noisy" scene with extra "Latin soul."

Casablanca   ▽ 23 | 16 | 21 | $22
3030 Severn Ave. (21st St.), 504-888-2209
"Delicious" Moroccan and even some "New York deli-type" dishes delight those who stumble on this "unique" Metairie eatery serving "excellent" kosher, dairy-free cuisine; the refurbished digs concealed within a "bland" exterior are decked with North African art, but more impressive to the lunch-hour set is the "fast service"; N.B. closed Friday nights and Saturdays until after sundown.

Casa Garcia   21 | 16 | 19 | $20
8814 Veterans Memorial Blvd. (David Dr.), 504-464-0354
Family-owned and "comfortable", this Metairie Mexican wraps up "always-fresh", "typical" dishes at "great prices"; its "super-friendly staff" is "usually quick", but "at peak times, you may have to wait" for a table (regulars recommend you indulge in a "big margarita" at the bar in the meantime).

Casamento's 🖻 Ⓜ ⇗   25 | 17 | 18 | $19
4330 Magazine St. (Napoleon Ave.), 504-895-9761;
www.casamentosrestaurant.com
Reviewers rave about the "exquisite oysters" – "briny and glistening on the half shell" or "fried to perfection" – and "amazing soft-shell crab po' boys" at this Uptown "old-schooler" (opened in 1919); if the "dazzling white tiles" strike some as "hospitallike" (made extra-stringent by "service with a frown"), it's also "as clean as an operating room" claim connoisseurs who recommend standing and "slurping at the bar"; P.S. it's closed on the off-season, "during months without an R."

CC's Gourmet Coffee House   19 | 17 | 19 | $7
Commons Shopping Ctr., 2917 Magazine St. (bet. 6th & 7th Sts.),
504-891-2115; www.ccscoffee.com
Latte lovers pour into this Louisiana chain's "traditional" cafes (a "fine alternative to Starbucks") for "don't-miss" Mochasipps, chicory coffee and "divine chocolate chip cookies" in the Garden District; "friendly baristas" keep the line moving, though nabbing a table among all the "students buried in their books" can be "tough."

CENTRAL GROCERY COMPANY 🖻 Ⓜ   24 | 13 | 16 | $12
923 Decatur St. (bet. Dumaine & St. Philip Sts.), 504-523-1620
"Gotta have the muffaletta" (an "unbeatable" sandwich of "huge" round loaves stuffed with meat, cheese and cracked olive salad) at this "most aromatic", century-old French Quarter Italian grocery store, known for inventing the delicacy; its minimal decor and "curt service" don't encourage lingering, so bag up the "classic" eats with some

"Zapp's chips and a Barq's root beer", then "head across the street and sit by the river for a true taste of the Big Easy."

Chateau Coffee Café 18 13 16 $12
3501 Chateau Blvd. (W. Esplanade Ave.), 504-465-9444
East Bank Regional Library, 4747 W. Napoleon Ave. (west of
Clearview Pkwy.), 504-888-0601
"Tasty breakfasts", "wonderful salads" and "white chocolate frozen coffee to die for" lure "leisurely" lunchers to these "peaceful" cafes in Kenner and Metairie; since you get a "good meal for money", it's easy for brew buffs of all budgets to "meet friends" and "relax the day away."

Chateau du Lac ⊠Ⓜ ▽ 25 18 23 $42
3901 Williams Blvd. (39th St.), 504-467-0054;
www.chateaudulacbistro.com
Although area francophones think this "authentic" "charming" "treasure" could use a more alluring location, they say it's "definitely worth the drive" to Kenner for the "excellent" "bistro fare" by a "true French chef"; sure, it's in a "strip mall of all places", but the inconvenience pays off if you "bring in their Web site coupon" for a "free bottle of wine."

China Doll ⊠ 21 14 19 $18
830 Manhattan Blvd. (Westbank Expwy.), 504-366-1700
"Chinese enough to feel like you're in China, American enough to feel at home", this West Banker's long been a favorite for "huge portions" of highly "craveable" Cantonese classics, including "outstanding General Tso's chicken"; definitely, "the decor needs a makeover", though.

Churros Café ⊠ − − − I
3100 Kingman St. (Veterans Memorial Blvd.), 504-885-6516
Sure, it's "nothing to look at – even feels like you're eating at Walgreen's, but the Cuban sandwiches are to die for" at this simple breakfast and lunch Metairie coffeehouse; they serve "great fruit shakes" too, "and you can't forget the churros", fried sugary pastries that are Spain's answer to the beignet.

Civello's ⊠Ⓜ**NEW** 22 25 25 $46
5831 Magazine St. (bet. Eleonore St. & Nashville Ave.),
504-899-6987
"Absolutely charming", this "intimate" "upscale Uptown Italian" (think fresh flowers, white tablecloths, candles and crystal chandeliers) is the town's "newest hot spot", "featuring opera-singing staffers" whose periodic arias "aren't nearly as annoying as you might think"; "now, if they could just make the food better" – while "authentic" enough, it's rather "average for the price."

CLANCY'S ⊠ 27 22 25 $45
6100 Annunciation St. (Webster St.), 504-895-1111
"Sublime smoked soft-shell crab" and "ooh-la-la" "oysters with Brie" among other "exquisite" dishes tantalize a

"tony", "table-hopping" "who's who" of "old New Orleans" at this "country club"–style Creole that some call the "Galatoire's of Uptown"; it can be "noisy and crowded" but "stands out as the quintessential locals' favorite", since it's "tucked away from all things touristy" and the "tuxedoed servers" have an "excellent rapport" with regulars.

Clementine's ☒ Ⓜ ∇ 24 21 21 $30
2505 Whitney Ave. (Fredericks St.), 504-366-3995
"Amazing" mussels/frites and other "authentic Belgian" bites, plus a "great selection of beers", make this "cozy, warm" West Bank bistro "worth going over the bridge" for – especially when such "delicious" food runs in the "middle price range"; its "new gallery setup" showcases furniture and art.

Clover Grill ◐ 18 14 17 $11
900 Bourbon St. (Dumaine St.), 504-598-1010;
www.clovergrill.com
"If you like service with attitude", "old-diner decor" and "drag queens cooking burgers" "under a '50s Cadillac hubcap", "this is your place" profess fans of this "funky" "staple of the Quarter" that's a "veritable culinary cabaret" 24/7; in fact, some are "convinced that the sauciness of the staff is the secret ingredient" of the "terrific", "greasy" grub.

Cochon ☒ NEW 25 22 23 $35
930 Tchoupitoulas St. (bet. Andrew Higgins Dr. & S. Diamond St.),
504-588-2123; www.cochonrestaurant.com
Locals "pigging out" on "tapas-style plates" of "authentic", pork-centric Cajun cuisine say "cheers for Donald Link" (also of Herbsaint), the chef/co-owner who fires up "dynamite" Southern Louisiana cooking inside this new Warehouse District "temple of swine"; the "fab" staff, open kitchen with wood-burning oven and "upscale-casual picnicky decor" guar-ontee it's a "real fun spot" to "bring a group of friends" and "sample a little of everything."

Coffea Coffeehouse Gallery ⌀ NEW – – – I
3218 Dauphine St. (bet. Louisa & Piety Sts.), 504-342-2484
Funk flourishes at this Bywater java joint and art gallery serving crêpes for breakfast and a variety of panini, tacos and salads for lunch; co-owners Andy and Gwen Forest (he's an artist and blues musician, she's the cook) have decorated the former furniture store with his paintings, her collection of religious objects and the offbeat creations of numerous friends; there's a small adjoining courtyard; N.B. serves food until 2 PM, open till 3 PM, closed Tuesdays.

Coffee Cottage 19 11 13 $14
5860 Citrus Blvd. (Dickory Ave.), 504-818-0051;
www.coffeecottage.com
Pastry chef/owner John Caluda's "cute little" Harahan coffee shop is a "really relaxing" place to have a "pleas-

ant" "chat with friends", preferably over a "scrumptious dessert", "consistently good lunch" or breakfast that's "served until noon on weekends (yes!)", offering ample time to taste "the most amazing grits you will ever put in your mouth."

Coffee Pot | 21 | 18 | 19 | $19 |

714 St. Peter St. (bet. Bourbon & Royal Sts.), 504-524-3500
"When you're in the Quarter and need to start the day (or soak up the night before)", check out this "old-school all the way" Creole-American whose "breakfast is the best" (and includes near-defunct, "historic dishes" like calas, or rice fritters); a "fairly priced" place, "it's strictly New Orleans in ambiance and soul", from the "attractive courtyard" to the "nice people."

Coffee Rani | 23 | 17 | 18 | $17 |

234A Lee Ln. (E. Boston St.), Covington, 985-893-6158
3517 Hwy. 190 (N. Causeway Blvd.), Mandeville, 985-674-0560
North Shore noshers know this pair of "go-to lunch spots" serves up the "best salads around", along with other "good, healthy food choices" that are a "reprieve from the city's artery-clogging staples"; they suggest you start with something "lo-cal or low-carb, and then blow your diet on one of the decadent desserts."

Come Back Inn ⊠ | 19 | 9 | 14 | $12 |

8016 W. Metairie Ave. (David Dr.), 504-467-9316
Feel like "you're back in the '50s" at this "order-at-the-counter", "kid-friendly" "locals hangout" in Metairie, which keeps 'em coming back for "quintessential New Orleans comfort food" (meaning meatball po' boys and veal cutlets "soggy with red gravy") plus American classics; as there's "no real decor", several "suggest taking it out."

Commander's Palace | – | – | – | E |

1403 Washington Ave. (Coliseum St.), 504-899-8221;
www.commanderspalace.com
Beautifully redecorated and more sumptuous than ever, with embroidered silk toile, wine leather banquettes and modern crystal chandeliers, this grand old Garden District star in the city's culinary cosmos (rated the Most Popular from 1989 through 2005) has finally reopened after a $6 million makeover in the wake of Katrina; its sophisticated Creole menu reflects the inventiveness of chef Tory McPhail, and its polished service shows the guidance of a new generation of Brennan ownership, cousins Lally Brennan and Ti Martin.

Coop's Place ● | ▽ 23 | 11 | 16 | $16 |

1109 Decatur St. (Ursulines Ave.), 504-525-9053;
www.coopsplace.net
A longtime late-nighters' and "locals' secret", this Quarter tavern dishes up "expertly prepared" Southern specialties

and "casual Cajun classics" to an "eclectic group of regulars and oddballs"; it's "killer food for a bar", but be prepared for a pretty "down-and-dirty" "dive"-like atmosphere ("the service and decor get better the more you drink", though).

Copeland's
18 | 16 | 16 | $27

680 N. Hwy. 190 (I-12), Covington, 985-809-9659
1700 Lapalco Blvd. (Manhattan Blvd.), Harvey, 504-364-1575
1534 Martin Luther King Jr. Blvd. (bet. Enterprise Dr. &
S. Hollywood Blvd.), Houma, 985-873-9600
www.alcopeland.com

Owned by Popeye's founder Al Copeland, this chain can be "excellent for out-of-towners if they want a good tour of Cajun-Creole food", served "with spice" in "wondrously extravagant portions"; but "bigger is not always better" say lachrymose locals lamenting the "hackneyed" eats (like "a Cajun TGI Friday's"); service and decor "need an upgrade as well."

Corky's Ribs & BBQ
19 | 13 | 17 | $16

4243 Veterans Memorial Blvd. (Houma Blvd.), 504-887-5000;
www.corkysbbq.com

Tennessee comes to Metairie at this rib shack, "an outpost of a Memphis-based chain"; aficionados ask "how can you beat" its "tender meats and sweet sauce" that offer "decent value for the money"?; while the simple setting will do "for a quick bite", many prefer the takeaway ("drive-thru BBQ — what a concept").

Country Flame
16 | 5 | 12 | $13

620 Iberville St. (Exchange Pl.), 504-522-1138

"Dark and dingy", this often crowded Cuban-Mexican Quarterite "is a real dive"; happily, the "authentic and filling" fajitas and flan at "basement prices" "taste better than the place looks."

COURT OF TWO SISTERS
19 | 24 | 21 | $40

613 Royal St. (bet. St. Peter & Toulouse Sts.), 504-522-7261;
www.courtoftwosisters.com

"Old-world decor", a "romantic" atmosphere and the "prettiest courtyard in the French Quarter" "take you back in time" at this stalwart septuagenarian famed for its daily jazz buffet brunch that's "fit for Bacchus" — and known to haul in the "cruise-ship masses"; a few find that since the post-Katrina chef change "it's on the upswing after years of decline", though many maintain that the Creole "cornucopia" impresses more for "the sheer volume of food than for quality", and the sisters are "resting firmly on their laurels."

Crabby Jack's ☒
26 | 9 | 14 | $13

428 Jefferson Hwy. (Knox Rd.), 504-833-2722

The "most creative po' boys" "on the planet" ("try the paneéd rabbit or braised duck" versions) and "fantastic fish tacos" keep this "ultracasual" Jefferson sandwich shop, "from the owner of Jacques-Imo's", filled with fans of its "awesome" plate lunches at "reasonable prices"; since there's usually a line, if you "don't want to wait" or "leave smelling like a fry cook", phone ahead for takeout.

Crazy Johnnie's Steakhouse   22 9 17 $21
3520 18th St. (N. Arnoult Rd.), 504-887-6641
"Even after an increase" in prices post-Katrina ("Johnnie's not as crazy as he used to be"), "steak lovers" still get a "great deal" at this Metairie meatery that serves up "moist, flavorful" filets "cooked to perfection"; "lots of locals" find it "a fun pace to go with friends", even if the staff "does try to rush you through" and the "decor's pretty plain" (despite a "recent remodel").

Crescent City Brewhouse   17 18 17 $24
527 Decatur St. (bet. St. Louis & Toulouse Sts.), 504-522-0571;
www.crescentcitybrewhouse.com
Tourists attest this "lively brewhouse" is the "perfect spot to rest your feet while sightseeing in the Quarter", especially on the balcony overlooking Decatur Street; if some joke they "remember the deck more than the food (what does that tell you?)", converts call the Contemporary Louisiana grub "quite good", if a tad "overpriced", and there's plenty of "nice cold beer" "handcrafted on-site."

Croissant d'Or Patisserie   25 18 18 $10
617 Ursuline Ave. (bet. Chartres & Royal Sts.), 504-524-4663
"Nothing changes it – not even a hurricane" or "new ownership" applaud *amis* of this Vieux Carré bakery/cafe, which provides *un peu de* "Paris in New Orleans" with "pastries in the true French style – so light and fluffy they float"; some come here "every morning" for the "best breakfast" on a covered "back patio with sparrows pecking around"; the lunchtime "sandwiches are a bargain" too.

Crystal Room   ▽ 20 20 19 $36
Le Pavillon Hotel, 833 Poydras St. (Baronne St.), 504-581-3111;
www.lepavillon.com
The "ornately decorated room" with its "Versaillesque" "high ceiling", marble floor and columns make this hotel CBDer a "classy, elegant" address for power meals – especially at midday, thanks to a newly enhanced lunch buffet whose Creole–New French fare is "fit for a king" (and "worth the expense").

Cuco's   13 12 13 $16
5048 Veterans Memorial Blvd. (bet. Kent Ave. &
Transcontinental Dr.), 504-454-5005 ⊠
Hammond Sq. Mall; 2000 SW Railroad Ave. (Minnesota Park Rd.),
Hammond, 985-345-2634
1300 Gause Blvd. (1 mile west of I-10), Slidell, 985-641-4706
"If you like Tex-Mex" and you're looking for "great value", you might fall for these "festive" cantinas and their "awe-

some" margaritas; more seasoned samplers sniff, however, this "run-of-the-mill chain" offers the "poorest excuse" for south-of-the-border *comidas* – "an American imitation of what they think Mexican food is."

CUVÉE ☒   28 26 26 $55
322 Magazine St. (bet. Gravier & Poydras Sts.), 504-587-9001; www.restaurantcuvee.com
Even in "the darkest days" just after Katrina, this Creole-Continental "shining light" in the CBD maintained "exceptional" standards, starting with chef Bob Iacovone's "outstanding", "creative" local cuisine with rich touches (e.g. "last meal"–worthy duck confit); the "wonderful" "French-focused wine list", "polished service" and "warm, dark decor" of gas lamps and exposed brick also help secure its rep as a "special-occasion" "gem."

DAKOTA, THE ☒   27 23 25 $49
629 N. Hwy. 190 (¼ mi. north of I-12), Covington, 985-892-3712; www.thedakotarestaurant.com
This Cuvée sibling wins accolades as the "most accomplished restaurant on the Northshore" thanks to its "excellent game", "fabulous crab and Brie soup" and other "decadent, delicious" New American–Contemporary Louisiana dishes; factor in "awesome wines", "exceptional service" and a setting enriched by deep colors and "great art on the walls" and most agree it's "worth the drive across the Causeway."

Dante's Kitchen   23 19 21 $32
736 Dante St. (River Rd.), 504-861-3121; www.danteskitchen.com
"Tucked-away" in Riverbend, this "charming" cottage wins praise for its "sophisticated" riffs on Creole–Contemporary Louisiana "comfort" fare, like "delicious" shrimp and grits, and "excellent" redfish on the half-shell; at Sunday brunch, everyone from "Uptown swells to jam band" players can be found "passing time with friends in the courtyard" and chatting with the "bohemian staff" – even if some say in summer the place swelters "like an inferno"; N.B. closed Tuesdays.

Deanie's Seafood   22 11 17 $22
1713 Lake Ave. (Live Oak St.), 504-831-4141; www.deanies.com
"Monstrous" "group-friendly" seafood platters and po' boys pack 'em in at this "noisy" Bucktown piscatorium, which "thrives on out-of-towners" and families; most find the service does not go so swimmingly, though, and cranky crustacean connoisseurs get "tired" of all the fried food, saying it's all about "quantity over quality" here.

Delachaise, The ☾   21 20 18 $23
3442 St. Charles Ave. (bet. Delachaise St. & Louisiana Ave.), 504-895-0858; www.thedelachaise.com
Whether it's a "bar that serves food or a restaurant with a bar" is open to interpretation, but most agree that since

this "hip" Uptown joint reopened in January 2006, chef Chris Debarr (formerly of the shuttered Christian's) has "worked wonders" in the kitchen with French-influenced bites ("divine" pommes frites "fried in duck fat") and "non-traditional tapas" that complement the "unique" wines; though some cite the bartenders for "snotty" treatment, that doesn't deter the clientele of "young single professionals."

DICK & JENNY'S ⊠ Ⓜ 27 | 21 | 24 | $37 |

4501 Tchoupitoulas St. (Jena St.), 504-894-9880; www.dickandjennys.com

Following what many call a "seamless" change of owners post-Katrina, this clapboard-cottage bistro on a "working-class" Uptown block remains "beloved" by locals thanks to "sumptuous", "soulful" Creole-Eclectic "comfort food" that "reflects the seasons" and comes at "very reasonable prices"; with the same "friendly" servers and "laid-back", "folk-art" atmosphere, it continues to draw fans who roll with the no-reserving policy by "lazing" away the "long waits" sipping drinks while "relaxing on the patio rockers."

DICKIE BRENNAN'S STEAKHOUSE 26 | 25 | 25 | $53 |

716 Iberville St. (bet. Bourbon & Royal Sts.), 504-522-2467; www.dickiebrennanssteakhouse.com

"Astounding steaks" "so tender they practically melt on the plate" wrangle French Quarter frequenters to this "beef eater's paradise" from the Brennan clan; the menu comes through with "all the extras" plus a "superior" wine selection, and the "clubby", "masculine" wood-paneled rooms, "well-trained" staff and hefty price tag are exactly what you'd expect "when you need that meat."

DiMartino's Muffulettas ⊠ 23 | 12 | 17 | $11 |

1788 Carol Sue Ave. (Wright Ave.), 504-392-7589
3900 General de Gaulle Dr. (Holiday Dr.), 504-367-0227

Worshipers "would cross the river just to get the muffaletta" (with "fresh ingredients" and an olive "kick") at this Algiers and Gretna deli duo serving the zesty sandwiches people "love"; "sloppy, sloppy" roast beef po' boys are also a hit, along with the family-friendly children's menu.

Domilise's Po-Boys ⊠⌀ 25 | 10 | 16 | $12 |

5240 Annunciation St. (Bellecastle St.), 504-899-9126

"Looks like a dump, tastes like a dream" crow crowds about this Cajun-Creole Uptown, whose po' boys are "best on the planet" – stuffed with "juicy" roast beef ("the gravy should be renamed New Orleans Holy Water"), "fresh" oysters ("fried as you watch") and other "fantastic" fillings on "perfect" bread; it's gotten "pricier", but otherwise older patrons swear "it hasn't changed" since they "snuck out of school 30 years ago" – certainly it seems like the "same ladies have been making the sandwiches since the beginning of time"; N.B. hours vary, so call ahead.

Dominique's 🈁Ⓜ   24 | 23 | 22 | $47

Maison Dupuy Hotel, 1001 Toulouse St. (bet. Burgundy & N. Rampart Sts.), 504-586-8000;
www.dominiquesrestaurant.com

"For a lighter touch", chef Dominique Macquet's "artistic" New French food with a "Caribbean influence" provides a "great change of pace", and convenient option for guests, at this French Quarter bistro in the Maison Dupuy; pleased patrons praise the "pampering staff", but a few claim the service and room ("plastic in feel") don't support the "high prices."

Dong Phuong   ∇ 22 | 11 | 15 | $16

14207 Chef Menteur Hwy. (Michoud Blvd.), 504-254-0296

This brave little lunch-only, family-style Vietnamese in New Orleans East is back up and running, serving an "exotic menu" with "wholesome pho" and "excellent" cold noodles and sandwiches to a primarily Asian clientele; the variety of desserts from its adjacent bakery is "not-to-be-missed."

Don's Seafood Hut   18 | 17 | 17 | $25

4801 Veterans Memorial Blvd. (Harvard Ave.),
504-889-1550

A suburban "staple", this longtime sib to the Lafayette original makes a "great gumbo" (order it with "extra oysters"), fries up "down-home", "delicious" "Acadiana-style" seafood for loyal families and "older" folks; fussier types find that despite an "updated look" post-Katrina, it's merely "average" and there are "better places in Metairie"; N.B. reservations are recommended.

Drago's 🈁   25 | 17 | 21 | $31

3232 N. Arnoult Rd. (bet. 17th & 18th Sts.), 504-888-9254;
www.dragosrestaurant.com

"You can't stop with the first dozen" "succulent" "charbroiled oysters", the "specialty" of this Metairie bivalve "master", which also offers less memorable seafood platters and "lobster dishes that won't break the bank"; while a recent renovation lends it a "trendier" feel, the "gracious staff" still "makes you feel right at home" – just be sure to "come early" or you can "expect to wait" since "no reservations" are the rule.

Dunbar's Creole Cooking 🈁   – | – | – | I

Loyola University Broadway Activities Ctr., 501 Pine St. (Dominican Ave.), 504-861-5451

Her unassuming, beloved Uptown Creole was shuttered due to Katrina damage, but determined owner Celestine Dunbar recently partnered with Loyola University's dining services to reopen as a public cafeteria-style stop on campus; in the spirit of old, specialties like fried chicken, mustard greens and red beans and rice are priced reasonably enough to keep students and their wallets full.

Eat ☒NEW   – | – | – | M
900 Dumaine St. (Dauphine St.), 504-522-7222
This strictly local, somewhat spartan Southerner with its
simple decor and amiable environment has won the hearts
of Quarterites for its down-home comfort dishes ranging
from grits and crawfish étouffée to burgers and bagels and
lox; neighbors want to keep this small spot to themselves,
especially for the budget-friendly weekend brunch.

Eleven 79 ☒   – | – | – | E
1179 Annunciation St. (Erato St.), 504-299-1179
Bravos broke out across town when this charming,
hidden-away old Warehouse District cottage reopened its
doors post-Katrina to dish up fabulous, garlicky Creole-
Italian pastas, veal and seafood courtesy of new chef
James Sibal; even though it costs lots of *lire,* the warm
brick walls and low lighting, a trendy bar and spot-on service are factors that fill it up fast.

Elizabeth's ☒   22 | 13 | 19 | $15
601 Gallier St. (Chartres St.), 504-944-9272;
www.elizabeths-restaurant.com
While some patrons still "miss Heidi", the latest owners of
this "sweet little" Bywater diner are maintaining its
"scrumptious" Southern "home cooking", plated up into
"hearty breakfasts" with "addictive praline bacon" on
the side; the addition of an upstairs bar means there's
one more reason for Bloody Mary brunchers to brave
the "run-down building."

EMERIL'S   25 | 24 | 25 | $59
800 Tchoupitoulas St. (Julia St.), 504-528-9393;
www.emerils.com
"Don't let the celebrity-chef status hold you back" say a
bevy of "bam!" believers who laud this Lagasse flagship in
the Warehouse District for "robustly flavored", "earthy"
eats that "capture the essence of New Orleans–style
haute cuisine"; its "crisp" service, "sleek" looks and high
energy ("the chef's bar is what I call 'dinner and a show'")
please most, though naysayers knock it as a "tourist
mecca" that needs to kick it "down a notch" in terms of
noise level and cost.

Emeril's Delmonico ☒☒   – | – | – | VE
1300 St. Charles Ave. (Erato St.), 504-525-4937;
www.emerils.com
Emeril Lagasse restored this century-old Lower Garden
District grande dame to its pre-Katrina glory, and after a
year's hiatus teams of waiters again prepare dishes tableside and piano players entertain in the clubby, elegant
space, which is decked with polished wood floors, plush
banquettes and large windows looking onto St. Charles
Avenue; the steaks are still dry-aged, the world-class wine

cellar – 6,000 bottles before the storm – is being rebuilt and the kitchen used the time off to create new dishes for the pricey menu of updated Creole classics.

Ernst Cafe ●   ▽ 12 | 11 | 15 | $14 |

600 S. Peters St. (Lafayette St.), 504-525-8544;
www.ernstcafe.net

This "funky Warehouse District" American built in 1902 is "busy at all hours" dispensing "typical" burgers and "loaded potatoes" for "mostly local businesspeople"; those unfazed by the original floor tiled with "inverted swastikas" (an ancient symbol that "stood for peace" and good luck pre–World War II) find the grub is "less than gourmet, but goes well with a draft Abita beer."

ETOILE ⊠   25 | 27 | 22 | $32 |

407 N. Columbia St. (E. Boston St.), Covington,
985-892-4578

The "arty, offbeat decor" with a "rustic touch" makes for "great ambiance" at artist James Michalopoulos' "hip", moderately priced New American–French bistro in Covington; most praise the menu as "ambitious", "eclectic" and "out of the ordinary", featuring "killer mussels" along with "fabulous" varietals from the attached wine shop.

Fausto's Bistro ⊠   21 | 14 | 19 | $27 |

(aka Fausto's Kitchen)
530 Veterans Memorial Blvd. (Aris Ave.), 504-833-7121

"Italian fare" meets "local flair" at this "consistent" Metairie mainstay serving "tender veal", "meaty lasagna" and "flavorful seafood"; though critics complain of rising prices and service that "needs improvement", the "small" space remains "crowded" with folks who say "give me great food over fancy decor any day."

Fazzio's ⊠   ▽ 20 | 12 | 18 | $27 |

1841 N. Causeway Blvd. (Hwy. 22), Mandeville,
985-624-9704

Pastas, steaks and salads in "large portions" bring North Shore value-seekers to this Mandeville Italian where "spaghetti and meatballs are a favorite", service is "friendly" and "noise from the bar" rarely abates.

Feelings Cafe Ⓜ   22 | 25 | 22 | $35 |

2600 Chartres St. (Franklin Ave.), 504-945-2222;
www.feelingscafe.com

Feelings indeed are aroused by the atmosphere ("I almost fell back in love with my old boyfriend") of this "intimate", "romantic" Creole-American "oasis" in a "historic" Marigny building with a "hidden jewel" of a patio bar; served by an "old-style staff", the "tasty" but "predictable" fare plays a minor role in the space's "Southern charm", which is so intoxicating that locals plead "don't publish" this one "because we want to keep it to ourselves."

Fellini's
19 | 15 | 17 | $16

900 N. Carrollton Ave. (City Park Ave.), 504-488-2147
Mid-City citizens appreciate the "veg"-friendly "variety"
at this "dependable" cafe that brings together "pizzas and
lavosh wraps to die for" among other Mediterranean eats;
its humble cafe setting is enhanced by sidewalk seating
and proximity to the New Orleans Museum of Art.

Fiesta Bistro NEW
∇ 17 | 15 | 18 | $19

1506 S. Carrollton Ave. (Jeannette St.), 504-865-1612
"A real sleeper", this "new addition" to Carrollton offers
"oodles of delicious", "reasonably priced" Spanish and
Mexican tapas; while the "casual" vibe has its appeal,
several say there are "still some kinks" – e.g. service that
ranges from "snappy" to "slow", and cuisine that's
"schizophrenic" qualitywise.

Fiesta Latina Ⓢ Ⓜ
– | – | – | I

1924 Airline Dr. (bet. Daniel & Minor Sts.), 504-469-5792
Homesick Hispanics and locals looking for "very authentic" Latin food head straight for this cavernous Kenner location to chow down on the real thing; conversation
competes with noisy piped-in music and Spanish-
language TV, so "if you're not into loud, order takeout."

Fiorella's Café
21 | 10 | 16 | $16

*1136 Decatur St. (bet. Governor Nicholls St. & Ursuline Ave.),
504-528-9566*
"Just like Sunday church, you have to wait an hour for the
chicken", the "famous" specialty of this "solid" soul food
and Southern Italian "find", but it's "worth it" for a fried-to-
order bird that poultry pundits progressively deem the
"best in the Quarter", "in NOLA" and "in the universe"; sure,
the place "looks like it's falling down", but that's just another reason it evokes the "New Orleans of 30 years ago."

Fire Ⓢ Ⓜ
– | – | – | E

*1377 Annunciation St. (Terpsichore St.), 504-566-1950;
www.firerestaurant.com*
Warehouse District diners blaze a trail to this lofty converted firehouse to get their fix of California-kissed New
American dishes prepared with locally grown ingredients;
along with a variety of braised and grilled chops, accents
like apricot-habanero dip and puttanesca flatbreads offer
a refreshing change from the traditional.

Five Happiness
22 | 19 | 22 | $20

3605 S. Carrollton Ave. (Palm St.), 504-482-3935
Sinophiles say this "immensely popular" Carrollton Chinese
sets the "gold standard" for Szechuan in the city, cooking
up a "consistent", "extensive menu" of "all the classic
Westernized dishes" at reasonable prices; the recently
renovated space is "usually packed and pleasantly noisy",

filled with "lots of families" and parties tended to by an "accommodating", kid-friendly staff.

Flaming Torch, The   20   21   19 $37
737 Octavia St. (bet. Constance & Magazine Sts.), 504-895-0900; www.flamingtorchnola.com
A "pleasant surprise" just off Magazine Street, this "little-known" Continental-French (with a "killer onion soup" among other "well-prepared" standards) is catching on with Uptown "ladies who lunch"; the "elegant", "well-appointed" candlelit dining room done up in a fiery red-brown and "reasonable" prices extinguish complaints of "uneven service."

Franky & Johnny's ⊠   19   10   17 $17
321 Arabella St. (Tchoupitoulas St.), 504-899-9146; www.frankyandjohnnys.com
"Come out smelling like you did the frying" at this "funky", "family-owned" Uptown Cajun "institution" whose "cheap" seafood (po' boys, crawfish), "cold beer" and a "great jukebox" make it the ultimate "down-home" "neighborhood dive"; killjoys claim they're "running on their reputation", but judging from the "long waits", it's "more popular than ever" – "just don't look at the floor."

Fresco Cafe   –   –   –   I
7625 Maple St. (Adams St.), 504-862-6363; www.frescocafe.us
University students and their Uptown neighbors go for the gourmet pies, Med apps and lavosh rolls, not to mention the Monday–Wednesday $2 pitchers of suds, in this modest pizzeria/cafe; a large sidewalk patio with ceiling fans for summer and heat lamps for cool days welcomes kids and dogs seven days a week.

Frosty's Café ⊠   ▽ 24   8   18 $15
3400 Cleary Ave. (bet. Veterans Memorial Blvd. & W. Esplanade Ave.), 504-888-9600
Feelings are anything but frosty when it comes to this tiny Metairie Vietnamese coffee shop whose "surprisingly good food" includes "great spring rolls" and "phenomenal bubble teas" in "any variation you can imagine"; add in a "patient" staff, and the only complaint is, "wish they had a larger eat-in area"; N.B. closes at 7 PM.

Fury's ⊠   23   11   18 $22
724 Martin Behrman Ave. (Veterans Memorial Blvd.), 504-834-5646
"Italian food like your grandma would make" (as well as "great fried chicken") are the hallmarks of this "old-fashioned" "no-nonsense" Metairie Italian-Creole "family restaurant" that's inhabited its strip-mall location "for many, many years"; a "pleasant atmosphere" and "friendly service" make it a "favorite with the over-70 crowd", so be advised: "go early or plan to wait."

GALATOIRE'S M
27 | 26 | 27 | $51

209 Bourbon St. (Iberville St.), 504-525-2021; www.galatoires.com
"You could see Blanche DuBois sipping a Sazerac" at this "old-line", "almost cultish" French Quarter centenarian – this city's Most Popular restaurant – a "'dress up and live large' kinda place" where "bigwigs" and "ladies in hats" find "gastronomic heaven" in a "classic" Creole-French cornucopia of "unbelievable seafood"; for best results, snag a table in the tiled downstairs room ("where the action is"), "get to know your waiter" and don't be surprised if a leisurely lunch "turns into dinner", especially on Fridays; N.B. jackets required after 5 PM and on Sundays.

Galley ☒M
24 | 11 | 19 | $21

2535 Metairie Rd. (Labarre Dr.), 504-832-0955
"A neighborhood classic", this Old Metairie "hole-in-the-wall" lures locals with "loaded plates" of the "freshest" boiled crawfish and a "fantastic" JazzFest-famous soft-shell crab po' boy, as well as other "fried and more fried" seafood; critics carp they're a "smidge overpriced", but that doesn't stop boatfuls lining up outside for "good eatin'"; P.S. regulars "love to dine on the porch."

GB's Patio Bar & Grill
17 | 14 | 18 | $15

8117 Maple St. (S. Carrollton Ave.), 504-861-0067
GB stands for "great burger" at this "unpretentious" Riverbend "joint" with a "delightful" "covered patio", "accommodating servers" and a crowd filled with families and "frat" types; however, detractors deem it merely "decent" claiming the quality "depends on how drunk you are."

Gordon Biersch
17 | 16 | 17 | $24

200 Poydras St. (S. Front St.), 504-552-2739; www.gordonbiersch.com
"If you've been to one, you've been to them all" say locals who find this "formulaic" American microbrewery in the CBD "fine" if you're looking for a "quick place" to "meet for a drink" of "handcrafted" suds; "food is not their strong point", though, and given its "restaurant-chain feel", most think "you can do better with a little searching."

Great Wall ☒
∇ 18 | 12 | 19 | $16

2023 Metairie Rd. (bet. Atherton Dr. & Helios Ave.), 504-833-2585
"Tucked away in Old Metairie", this venerable Chinese is (and "always has been") "a gem" for Mandarin mavens who maintain it has some of the "best egg rolls", General Tso's chicken and other standards; all's served in "quiet", if simple family-friendly surroundings.

Gulfstream St. Charles NEW
20 | 21 | 19 | $36

1755 St. Charles Ave. (Felicity St.), 504-524-1578
The "transformation of this former Houston's" into a new "seafood-oriented" Contemporary Louisiana place "run by

the same company" meets with mixed reviews; converts call it "a fine addition to St. Charles Avenue", with a "more upscale" aura and "well-prepared offerings", but skeptics lament it "lacks soul and character" (at least, the "rushing" servers do), labeling the food "overpriced and unnecessarily pretentious."

Gumbo Shop   22 | 18 | 20 | $22 |
630 St. Peter St. (bet. Chartres & Royal Sts.), 504-525-1486; www.gumboshop.com

"Ignore the grungy surroundings and laid-back service": this French Quarter Creole is still the spot for its "awesome" namesake soup (in meat and vegetarian varieties), plus "perfect" red beans and rice and bread pudding – and "at low prices" too; yes, it attracts a lot of tourists – and often gets "mobbed" with 'em, in fact – but even locals admit that this longtime "favorite" is frequently "busy for a reason."

GW Fins   25 | 25 | 24 | $49 |
808 Bienville Ave. (bet. Bourbon & Dauphine Sts.), 504-581-3467; www.gwfins.com

"Fabulous", "fresh" fish dishes of "almost every type" – that don't tow the traditional New Orleans line – fill the plates at this large seafooder, which is just as memorable for its "addictive" "hot biscuits"; service is "mature" and "top-notch", and though some find the "sleek", "open" dining room "a little mainstream for the French Quarter", most feel it lives up to the "swanky price."

Hana Japanese   20 | 14 | 17 | $22 |
8116 Hampson St. (S. Carrollton Ave.), 504-865-1634

"If I were on death row, I'd eat my last meal here" effuse fin-atics of this "tiny" Riverbend spot and its "melt-in-your-mouth" "sushi New Orleans–style" ("love the fried softshell crab roll") "beautifully presented" by chef Taisuke Tomiyama; manager Kazuyo (his wife) keeps the vibe "informal", so even if foes find the space "cheesy" and the sushi merely "serviceable", most are taken with the "lively" atmosphere.

HANSEN'S SNO-BLIZ Ⓜ⇗   29 | 16 | 22 | $4 |
4801 Tchoupitoulas St. (Bordeaux St.), 504-891-9788

"Here's to another generation" say devotees delighted that Ashley Hansen has revived this Uptown "New Orleans classic" stand after the passing of her grandparents; voted top Bang for the Buck, it delivers the "ultimate" "warm-weather treats" – "delicacies" of finely shaved ice with the "consistency of a snowflake", topped by a variety of "homemade flavors"; even after a "45-minute wait", refreshed fans say "try one, you'll be spoiled" by this "Antoine's of sno-balls"; N.B. hours are seasonal and limited (most recently Friday–Sunday), so call ahead.

Harbor Seafood & Oyster Bar   23 | 9 | 16 | $16
3203 Williams Blvd. (32nd St.), 504-443-6454
Shell-shuckers crack into this "oysterrific" Kennerite for "mouthwatering" boiled and fried seafood chased by an "ice-cold beer"; despite its "small", "nothing-to-look-at" digs "near the airport", the "freshest" catches in the Gulf – including "super crawfish", "salty oysters" and fine "fried alligator" – at "affordable prices" help keep it "packed."

Hard Rock Cafe   13 | 21 | 15 | $24
418 N. Peters St. (St. Louis St.), 504-529-5617; www.hardrock.com
"Why would anyone come here in NOLA?" ask exasperated eaters about this "expensive", "memorabilia-covered" outpost of the national rock 'n' roll chain; the answer is, it's "cheerful", "loud" and "exciting" for tourists and "groups of kids or young execs", the burger-centric food is "better than you'd expect" and some just feel compelled to "go to Hard Rocks everywhere", if only "for the T-shirts and drinks."

HERBSAINT ⬧   27 | 22 | 25 | $45
701 St. Charles Ave. (Girod St.), 504-524-4114; www.herbsaint.com
In "top form" post-Katrina, the kitchen at this Warehouse District "winner" turns out "stellar" New American–French fare with a "Southern twist" and a touch of "whimsy", thanks to "truly talented" chef Donald Link; its "chic" dining room is both "casual" and "electric", energized by "enticing" cocktails, a "wonderful wine list" and "smart service" – in sum, "another home run" from co-owner Susan Spicer.

Hillbilly BBQ ⬧ Ⓜ   24 | 9 | 16 | $13
208 Tullulah Ave. (Jefferson Hwy.), 504-738-1508
Pit-"masters" Kelly Moskaw and Larry Wyatt's "smoky and tender" brisket, ribs and other hickory-fired meats, plus "delicious sides" distinguish this "unpretentious", "rustic" River Ridge BBQ "joint"; in a town not known for authentic 'cue, those looking for the "real deal" say this is "as good as it gets in New Orleans."

Home Furnishings Store Cafe ⬧⬦   ▽ 18 | 11 | 16 | $11
1600 Prytania St., 2nd fl. (Terpsichore St.), 504-566-1707
"Tucked away on the second floor" of a Lower Garden District furniture store, this "hidden" Creole-American lunch nook serves a "great chunky chicken salad" and other refueling fare from the "tiny kitchen" of chef Gloria Allen; bemused sofa shoppers swear its "stepping-into-the-late-'70s" ambiance suits the "odd, eccentric" locale perfectly.

Horinoya ⬧   24 | 18 | 20 | $28
920 Poydras St. (bet. Baronne St. & O'Keefe Ave.), 504-561-8914
There's "never a crowd" at this "secret" Japanese in the CBD, praised by "neo-Nippon" enthusiasts for its "high-

quality", "competently" prepared sushi and "non-Americanized", "authentic" appetizers; complementing the clean cuisine are a "streamlined" look and "attentive" servers, particularly those who "know their customers."

Houston's   21   19   20 $27

4241 Veterans Memorial Blvd. (Clearview Pkwy.), 504-889-2301; www.houstons.com

"Always reliable", this "crazy popular" "upscale" American franchise serves "steady cookie-cutter cuisine" (plus "great spinach dip") in Metairie; service is a "strength", though many "sorely miss" the Lower Garden District location (morphed by management into Gulfstream St. Charles), and others gripe the "waits are frustrating" and it's "way too expensive for a hanging-fern chain."

Ignatius Eatery NEW   –   –   –   I

4200 Magazine St. (Milan St.), 504-896-2225

Gumbo, muffalettas and po' boys plump up the Creole menu at this casual new Uptowner, named for the corpulent Crescent City protagonist of *A Confederacy of Dunces*; the premises look like an old mom-and-pop corner grocery, with iconic Louisiana products stacked against the walls (all for sale), alongside the spirited sign 'if it ain't New Orleans, we ain't got it' – and they mean it.

Impastato's ☒ Ⓜ   24   18   22 $36

3400 16th St. (bet. N. Hullen St. & Severn Ave.), 504-455-1545; www.impastatos.com

"In 20 years, never had a bad meal" here proclaim parish paisans of this "old-style" suburbanite in Metairie ("hard to find" but "worth the effort"), whose "Creole-influenced" Italian menu contains "more food than you can handle"; the "excellent" service under congenial chef-owner Joe Impastato, plus nightly sets by the "old guy singing karaoke", add some glitz to a "no-flair" interior.

IRENE'S CUISINE ☒   26   22   23 $41

539 St. Philip St. (Chartres St.), 504-529-8811

"Locals love" this "dark", "romantic" trattoria that tourists seem to "find with their noses" as the scent of "delectable" Southern Italian food permeates its French Quarter block; inside, "cozy, quirky" dining rooms, a "delightful staff" and "great piano bar" keep spirits soaring – but since no reserving can mean "painful" waits, you'd best show up early, add your name to the list and "take the opportunity" to explore the area.

Iris ☒ NEW   25   19   23 $40

8115 Jeannette St. (S. Carrollton Ave.), 504-862-5848; www.irisneworleans.com

Chef Ian Schnoebelen and co-owner Laurie Casebonne (both ex Lilette) make this new Carrollton "gem" "shine", serving "fresh", "imaginative" New American meals – not to mention "superb martinis"; early-comers add that the "small but charming" cottage setting and "knowledgeable staff" heighten the appeal of this "hot" spot that's "quickly become a local favorite."

Italian Pie 17 | 9 | 12 | $14 |

4840 Bienville Ave. (N. Anthony St.), 504-483-9949
5650 Jefferson Hwy. (Evans Rd.), 504-734-3333
417 S. Rampart St. (Perdido St.), 504-522-7552
3600 Williams Blvd. (W. Esplanade Ave.), 504-469-4999
1319 Gause Blvd. (Eastridge Dr.), Slidell, 985-661-0240
www.italianpierestaurants.com
"It's a pizza joint" without pretension, so the "creative", "dependable" pies tend to satisfy families, "business crowds" and delivery devotees of this Southern chain; the salads and calzones also have their fans, though "slow, inexact service" and "no atmosphere" further dissuade those who say "Katrina blew the good food away."

Jack Dempsey's ⊠ M 21 | 12 | 19 | $19 |

738 Poland Ave. (Dauphine St.), 504-943-9914
"Seriously fried fish" and baked macaroni fit for heavyweights reign "supreme" at this "frozen-in-time" Bywater seafood house where each "heaping plate" "could feed two hungry longshoremen"; service is "usually good" and despite the "hard-to-find", "cramped" space, the hook is "it hasn't changed in decades."

Jackson NEW 20 | 20 | 23 | $42 |

1910 Magazine St. (St. Mary St.), 504-529-9599;
www.jacksonnola.com
Set in a historic building with exposed brick and a "balcony dining" area, this Lower Garden District "post-Katrina newcomer" melds an "innovative" menu of Contemporary Louisiana cuisine with old-world but "unpretentious" service; oenophiles applaud its "not overpriced" wine list and "killer" boozy brunch and just hope it will triumph in some youthful "struggles with consistency."

JACQUES-IMO'S CAFE ⊠ 27 | 21 | 22 | $33 |

8324 Oak St. (S. Carrollton Ave.), 504-861-0886;
www.jacquesimoscafe.com
Fans of Jack Leonardi's "big-flavored", "down-home" Creole soul cooking at this Carrollton "dive" assure you'll be "sighing in bliss and loosening your pants" before you can say "alligator cheesecake" (a "must-try"); sure, many bemoan the "insanely long" waits that can run over an hour, but even so most call this "funky", "boisterous" "Tulane students' fave" "a blast" that "could only exist in New Orleans."

Jamila's Cafe M 22 | 16 | 24 | $27 |

7808 Maple St. (Burdette St.), 504-866-4366
Most reviewers "can't say enough" about this "warm, inviting" Uptowner whose highly "personal touch" comes

courtesy of "attentive" owners Jamila and Moncef Shaa; chef Jamila creates "excellent" renditions of "unique" Tunisian and Med specialties, and weekend belly dancers and flamenco guitarists make this an all-around "great" "go-to" place; N.B. a recent redo may outdate the Decor score.

Jazmine Café Ⓜ   18   12   17 $13
614 S. Carrollton Ave. (St. Charles Ave.), 504-866-9301
This "tasty" Vietnamese-Eclectic draws in Carrollton college kids and other locals looking for "value" with its "inexpensive" tabs, "many vegetarian options" and "very good" bubble teas; it's "nothing fancy" – in fact, the setting's "a bit sterile" – but "recommended for a casual meal."

Jazz Tacos ⇗ NEW   –   –   –   I
307 Exchange Alley (bet. Chartres & Royal Sts.), 504-872-0015
One of the few places with sidewalk tables in the French Quarter, this little newcomer serves up simple, straightforward Honduran and Central American dishes like fajitas, pupusas and tamales in addition to its specialty tacos; the chef uses no lard in the beans and makes everything from scratch, including chips and salsa; N.B. closes around 8 PM.

Jipang Ⓩ   –   –   –   I
814 Gravier St. (bet. Baronne & Carondelet Sts.),
504-565-5322
The CBD lunch bunch have honed in on this "stylish" weekday Japanese serving "zippy" and "delicious" noodle dishes and "always fresh" sushi; "bargain" prices and "friendly" service make up for oddball hours (closes at 2:30 PM).

Joey K's Ⓩ   17   11   17 $16
3001 Magazine St. (7th St.), 504-891-0997;
www.joeyksrestaurant.com
Nothing could be "more New Orleans" than this Garden District "icon" serving Creole "comfort food" including "plate lunch specials", "all-you-can-eat catfish" and "frosty" schooners of Abita; the decor is "quirky" at best, "run-down" at worst, but this "local joint" is one of the "great melting pots in the city", where "businessmen, plumbers and families all eat together."

Joint, The Ⓩ   25   15   22 $12
4113 Magazine St. (Miland St.), 504-899-4227 NEW
801 Poland Ave. (Dauphine St.), 504-949-3232
'Cue connoisseurs seeking "barbecue bliss" find it at this "funky" Bywater joint featuring "fantastic" pulled pork, "finger-lickin' good" ribs and a "mouthwatering" lineup of sides; a "local vibe" and the "best jukebox in the city" ensure this "really cool" joint is "always smokin'"; N.B. heads up, Uptowners: a take-out shop has opened on Magazine Street.

Juan's Flying Burrito ⊠   22 14 16 $14
2018 Magazine St. (bet. Josephine & St. Andrew Sts.),
504-569-0000
4724 S. Carrollton Ave. (Canal St.), 504-486-9950
www.juansflyingburrito.com
"Creatively filled" burritos "as big as your head" keep
these "loud" Lower Garden District and Mid-City Mexican-
Creole taquerias packed with "young broke hipsters"
seeking "fresh" takes on "cheap eats"; however, given
the "scary" decor and a "surly" tattooed staff, you may
want to keep the "potent" margaritas coming, or "get your
order to go."

Kim Son ⊠   25 13 19 $20
349 Whitney Ave. (Westbank Expwy.), 504-366-2489
This "family-run", "authentic" Asian is known for its "fresh
ingredients" and "unbelievable" "salt-baked seafood
dishes" that reward "a trip across the river" to Gretna;
regulars recommend you "stick to the Vietnamese specialties" ("not the Chinese"); and if you don't warm to the
staff's "detached competence" and "decor that needs improvement", just keep in mind the low cost.

Kosher Cajun NY Deli & Grocery   ▽ 21 10 20 $13
3519 Severn Ave. (W. Esplanade Ave. S.), 504-888-2010;
www.koshercajun.com
There's no place in town more "like a New York deli" than
this "awesome" Metairie nosh shop serving "Jewish favorites", from corned beef on rye with Dr. Brown's cream
soda, to matzo ball soup "you'll love", to "kosher gumbo
(don't know how they do it!)"; groceries "by the pound"
enhance the offerings of this plain, "family-operated"
eatery; N.B. closed Saturdays, open for Passover.

K-PAUL'S LOUISIANA KITCHEN ⊠   27 21 24 $48
416 Chartres St. (bet. Conti & St. Louis Sts.), 504-596-2530;
www.kpauls.com
"Not the cliché you'd expect", the French Quarter birth-
place of blackened redfish maintains high standards
thanks to "flavor virtuoso" Paul Prudhomme and his "complex, sophisticated interpretation" of "robustly" spiced
Cajun food; "long waits" are often a prelude to the "hot
and pricey" fare, but "spirited" service and a "charming",
"casual" atmosphere that encourages "talking to people
you don't know" help ensure "a good time."

Kyoto ⊠   23 17 18 $25
4920 Prytania St. (bet. Robert & Upperline Sts.), 504-891-3644
"Inventive" combinations that "hit the mark every time"
distinguish the "consistent, fresh" sushi sliced up at this
"reasonably priced" Uptown Japanese; insiders applaud
the "must-try" spicy Sara roll (shrimp and chile sauce) as
well as "unlisted" catches that the "caring staff" will rec-

ommend if you ask; the "space is small", but "sitting at the bar" with the "entertaining chefs" is a kick.

Kyoto II   ∇ 20 | 14 | 19 | $24
Citrus Palm Shopping Ctr., 5608 Citrus Blvd. (Kuebel St.), 504-818-0228
Unrelated to the Uptown Kyoto, this six-year-old Harahan Japanese tucked in the Citrus Palm Shopping Center produces "dependable", "quality sushi" "for the 'burbs", with a "large selection" and "inexpensive" lunch specials, making it a welcome stop for those who live in River Ridge or work at Elmwood; "pleasant, knowledgeable chefs" and "attentive" staffers help keep the fairly "bland" room "packed."

La Boca ⌧ NEW   – | – | – | E
857 Fulton St. (St. Joseph St.), 504-525-8205
In good weather, they throw the doors open at this compact Argentine steakhouse in the Warehouse District, an upscale newcomer from the owners of RioMar decorated with soccer photos and uniforms from Buenos Aires; the menu packs a rarefied red meat kick, boasting more than a dozen cuts of steak served with a real char on them, and Argentine and Italian wines that can be ordered by the half bottle.

LA BOULANGERIE ⌿   28 | 19 | 19 | $9
4526 Magazine St. (Jena St.), 504-269-3777
"Wonderful, freshly baked breads", including "airy baguettes" and "excellent buns", are "the reason to go" to this "incredible bakery" Uptown – though the "heavenly pastries" and "King Cakes during Carnival" have their champions too; "charming", "very French" and furnished with a few tables, its only difference from a "perfectly typical" Parisian *pâtisserie* is the "Southern drawl" of the staff.

La Côte Brasserie   23 | 24 | 23 | $43
Renaissance Arts Hotel, 700 Tchoupitoulas St. (Girod St.), 504-613-2350; www.lacotebrasserie.com
"Slick", "modern" and "open"-feeling, this "excellent" upscale Creole-French brasserie inside the Warehouse District's Renaissance Arts Hotel offers an "unexpected" menu of "savory, seasonal creations"; the "great Sunday brunch" and an "informed staff" boost its appeal "to all taste buds", not only those of the "hotel-based" tourists.

La Crêpe Nanou ⌧ M   24 | 23 | 21 | $31
1410 Robert St. (Prytania St.), 504-899-2670
For a "total French immersion", Uptowners "don't mind waiting" in line at this "casual but elegant" bistro for dishes like "not-to-be-missed" mussels and frites, and "delicious" dessert crêpes; "ideal for dates" and sidewalk dining, it's "affordable" to boot, and if the waiters are a little "surly", that's "just like Paris" too; N.B. closed Sundays and Mondays.

La Louisiane ◗   ▽ 18 20 17 $45
725 Iberville St. (bet. Bourbon & Royal Sts.), 504-378-8200;
www.lalouisiane.com
Vintage-looking gold-leaf details meet "sensual", even
steamy, artwork at this French Quarter celebration site,
which has lived many lives since 1881 (with a hiatus from
1996 to 2004); most find the staff satisfactory, though opinions
differ on Contemporary Louisiana dishes, among them beer-
braised short ribs and saffron-spiced bouillabaisse, which
some call "fantastic" and others deem "disappointing."

La Madeleine French Bakery   20 17 15 $15
Elmwood Shopping Ctr., 5171 Citrus Blvd. (Clearview Pkwy.),
504-818-2450
601 S. Carrollton Ave. (St. Charles Ave.), 504-861-8661
www.lamadeleine.com
Only the Harahan and Riverbend locations of this "cafeteria-
style" French bistro/bakery chain have reopened since
Katrina, but both continue to draw fans of its "amazingly
versatile kitchen", which offers "affordable", "consistent
and copious" eats, such as "great soups", "fresh salads"
and "luscious desserts", particularly the "addictive"
strawberries Romanoff; though the staff is just "ok", it
keeps a "quick" pace.

Landry's Seafood House   15 16 16 $29
400 N. Peters St. (Conti St.), 504-558-0038;
www.landrysseafood.com
"Trying to pass itself off as a traditional NOLA" place, this
sprawling branch of a Texas-based outfit appeals to the
"tour-bus crowd" with live music, an accessible Quarter location and "decent" fried, boiled and baked seafood in servings "so large you can't finish them"; purists, however, holler
"stay away" from this "corporate" contender – "you're in
New Orleans, why are you eating at a chain restaurant?"

La Petite Grocery ☒ Ⓜ   26 24 24 $45
4238 Magazine St. (General Pershing St.), 504-891-3377
Raves abound for chef Anton Schulte (ex Peristyle and
Clancy's) and his "welcome addition to Uptown", serving
"sophisticated", "inventive" Contemporary Louisiana–
French cuisine amid "understated" surroundings in a renovated former corner grocery; despite "the din", fans find
it a "perfect blend of special-occasion restaurant and
neighborhood bistro", whose "simple" "Parisian style",
"polished service" and "blissful" bites make you think
"you're on the Left Bank."

LA PROVENCE Ⓜ   27 26 26 $46
25020 Hwy. 190 (bet. Lacombe & Manderville), Lacombe,
985-626-7662; www.laprovencerestaurant.com
After 34 years, "treasured" toque Chris Kerageorgiou still
turns out "superb" French "comfort food to die for" at this

unexpected "bit of Provence" on a highway in rural Lacombe; "romantic" meals "you'll remember for a lifetime" are enhanced by "lovely hearth fires" and "welcoming" service, and the three-course prix fixe offers "excellent value"; N.B. closed Mondays and Tuesdays.

La Thai Cuisine ⓈE
23 | 17 | 21 | $31

933 Metairie Rd. (Rosa Ave.), 504-828-3080

Folks are happy to Thai one on at this Old Metairie fusion "find", which serves "generous portions" of "innovative", "well-seasoned" Siamese-Cajun cooking; though some say it's "a bit pricey for what you get", others praise its "relaxing" atmosphere that's refined enough "for a nice night out."

Laurentino's Barcelona Tapas ⓈE
▽ 25 | 14 | 20 | $28

4410 Transcontinental Dr. (W. Esplanade Ave.),
504-779-9393

This "hidden gem" in a Metairie strip mall attracts regulars who savor its "authentic Spanish" specialties, including tapas, cooked up Catalan-style; "awesome sangria" and a "personable staff" help make diners "feel at home"; N.B. recent renovations, including the addition of a patio, may outdate the Decor score.

Lebanon's Café
23 | 15 | 17 | $16

1500 S. Carrollton Ave. (Jeannette St.), 504-862-6200

"College folks" and meze mavens love the Lebanese feasts at this "hopping" Carrollton "hangout" where the "flavorful" falafel, hummus and lamb come in "huge portions" that are "cheap as all get out"; the surrounds are "a step up from diner decor" (with "alfresco" seating), service is "friendly" and even though it's BYO, the "not-too-sweet" Lebanese iced tea makes a fine, "thirst-quenching tonic."

Le Citron Bistro ⓈM
– | – | – | I

1539 Religious St. (Orange St.), 504-566-9051

An 1810 building with its original brick walls and exposed beams houses this way-off-the-beaten-path Warehouse District establishment, overflowing into a charming muralled patio; chef-owner David Baird's menu features affordable versions of Creole and Italian fare, along with a few sandwiches to match a drink at the bar; N.B. open Wednesday through Saturday only.

Lee's Hamburgers
21 | 9 | 15 | $9

904 Veterans Memorial Blvd. (Oaklawn Dr.), 504-836-6804
4301 Veterans Memorial Blvd. (Houma Blvd.), 504-885-0110 ⌐

"Dreamy", "old-fashioned hamburgers" with caramelized "cooked-in onions", "excellent" onion rings and cheese fries are a "revelation" for fans of this "very '50s" Metairie pair (the only branches to survive post-Katrina); while they're just a couple of counter-service "joints", the quality is so "great" that worshipers wonder how "all those national chains are still in business."

Le Parvenu ⊠   26 │ 24 │ 23 │ $38 │
509 Williams Blvd. (bet. Kenner Ave. & Short St.), 504-471-0534
Urbanites ask "who knew?" about this "quaint" "little"
"charmer" in Kenner serving "terrific", "intriguing" New
American–Creole dishes, particularly the signature
paneéd lobster; though some think it's "high-priced for the
'burbs", most find it an "unexpected joy" for "relaxing" in
a "lovely" cottage setting – particularly on the "delightful
porch" for brunch.

Liborio Cuban Restaurant ⊠   22 │ 14 │ 16 │ $20 │
321 Magazine St. (bet. Canal & Poydras Sts.), 504-581-9680;
www.liboriocuban.com
It's "worth a walk in the sultry summer heat" to find this
CBD "respite" for "bountiful plates" of "earthy", "garlicky"
Cuban-Spanish fare, served at a "leisurely" pace; the
lively lime-green walls also "refresh" the clientele on their
office breaks, so even if it "always seems to cost more
than it should", it's worth it to feel you've "died and gone
to Cuba"; N.B. dinner Thursday–Saturday only.

Li'l Dizzy's Cafe ⊠   – │ – │ – │ I │
1500 Esplanade Ave. (N. Robertson St.), 504-569-8997
Neighborhood folks and a few savvy tourists crowd this
"essential" Mid-City Creole cafe, where chef-owner
Wayne Baquet (whose daddy ran the famous Eddie's)
dishes up "stick-to-your-ribs soul food" for a wallet-
friendly breakfast or lunch; though Katrina wreaked havoc
with the roof and looters made off with the Dizzy Gillespie
portrait, the place has bounced back, buoyed by lots
of "community support."

LILETTE ⊠Ⓜ   26 │ 23 │ 23 │ $46 │
3637 Magazine St. (Antonine St.), 504-895-1636;
www.liletterestaurant.com
Whether for an "intimate dinner" or "sybaritic lunch", this
"top-tier" French Uptowner impresses with "inventive
combinations" of "fresh seasonal ingredients" by "brilliant" chef-owner John Harris; "chic" yet "relaxed", it
draws "young professionals" and other locals who "love
the booths" as well as the "cool bar" (complete with "sexy
drinks"), all tended by a "friendly", "unrushed" staff.

Little Tokyo   22 │ 13 │ 19 │ $23 │
1521 N. Causeway Blvd. (bet. 43rd & 44th Sts.),
504-831-6788 ◗
590 Asbury Dr. (Desoto St.), Mandeville, 985-727-1532
These Japanese sibs in Metairie and Mandeville "satisfy"
with "reliable" "fresh sushi" ("swamp rolls rule!") and
"quick, courteous" service; they're low on "ceremony"
and "fancy-dancy" decor, but that doesn't keep diners
from willingly "waiting for a table", particularly at the
smaller Asbury Drive locale.

Liuzza's by the Track ⌺ 24 | 12 | 18 | $15
1518 N. Lopez St. (Ponce de Leon St.), 504-218-7888
"Oh my, *cher!*" say lovers of this "legendary watering
hole" in Mid-City, who go for the "best damn gumbo" and
"must"-have po' boys stuffed with "succulent" garlic oysters or BBQ shrimp, and washed down with their famed
Bloody Marys or "iced schooners of beer"; sure, this
Creole is "not much of a place" decorwise, but it'll still wet
everyone's whistle after "an afternoon at the racetrack" or
"on the way to JazzFest."

Liuzza's Restaurant & Bar ⌺ Ⓜ 21 | 14 | 20 | $17
3636 Bienville Ave. (N. Telemachus St.), 504-482-9120;
www.liuzzas.com
After draining six feet of water from the dining room, this
'40s-era Creole-Italian "classic" "neighborhood tavern" in
Mid-City is back; the menu's slightly abbreviated, but "they
still fry everything perfectly", including "heavenly" onion
rings, and serve the original 'Frenchuletta' sandwich (a
muffaletta on French) plus "frosty mugs" of beer; with its
"hard-working" staff and "homey" atmosphere, locals liken
it to "an old shoe – doesn't look great but feels wonderful."

Lola's ⇭ 26 | 19 | 21 | $26
3312 Esplanade Ave. (bet. N. Broad & N. Carrollton Aves.),
504-488-6946
Iberia buffs "wish there were more" "warm", "lovely little"
"date" spots like this inexpensive Mid-City "delight",
which serves "authentic" Spanish dishes such as "top-
notch pork loin" and "paella that rocks"; the no-reserving
policy translates into patrons "waiting outside in lounge
chairs" and "sipping the wine they've brought for dinner",
gearing up for a glorious "garlic experience" – "vampires
beware"; N.B. the house now offers beer, wine and sangria in addition to welcoming BYO.

Longbranch, The Ⓜ NEW ▽ 26 | 26 | 22 | $55
21516 Hwy. 36 (Hwy. 59), Abita Springs, 985-871-8171
"Rising culinary stars" and married chefs Allison Vines-
Rushing and Slade Rushing (both ex Jack's Luxury Oyster
Bar, NYC) craft "cutting-edge", "brilliantly executed" New
French food at this Abita Springs "destination" housed in
a "beautiful" former 19th-century hotel; the veranda and
garden (complete with a cat) enhance the "charming" atmosphere, so the "pricey" menu and occasionally "spotty"
service" barely ruffle any feathers.

Louisiana Pizza Kitchen 20 | 15 | 17 | $18
95 French Market Pl. (Barracks St.), 504-522-9500
615 S. Carrollton Ave. (St. Charles Ave.), 504-866-5900
If it's "crisp" "wood-fired pizzas" with "nouveau" combinations of "local ingredients" you "crave", this "dependable" Italian duo, which serves pastas and salads as well,

just might "hook" you; the Riverbend location feels "chainy"-trendy, while the Quarter branch offers sidewalk seating to catch the "French Market bustle."

Lucy's Retired Surfer's   14 14 15 $17
Bar & Restaurant
701 Tchoupitoulas St. (Girod St.), 504-523-8995;
www.lucysretiredsurfers.com
"Decent" Cal-Mex "bar food" and "cool" cocktails round out this "laid-back" "watering hole" in the Warehouse District, a "sweet retreat" for lunch or after-work drinks and apps; the "bad but inventive" decorations help the place "live up to its irreverent name", and if some are there mostly to ogle the "eye candy" waitresses, who did you expect at this boozy "fun dump"?

Madrid Ⓜ   ▽ 19 12 18 $33
2723 Roosevelt Blvd. (bet. 27th St. & Veterans Blvd.), 504-469-5599
"Don't be fooled by outside appearances" say Kennerites who've discovered the "fresh", "top-notch" tapas, along with some of "the best paella in town", at this strip-mall Spanish cafe; just keep in mind that this plain-Juanita probably isn't the setting for a marriage proposal.

Maple Street Cafe   22 18 19 $27
7623 Maple St. (bet. Adams & Hillary Sts.), 504-314-9003
A "mix of young and old", from "students and their families" to "ladies who lunch", dote on the "delicious", "cosmopolitan" and "reasonably" priced cuisine at this "cozy" Italian-Med in Carrollton; its "inviting", "sweetly romantic" dining room and patio are pleasers, though some say service could be better paced.

Marigny Brasserie   22 23 21 $36
640 Frenchmen St. (Royal St.), 504-945-4472;
www.cafemarigny.com
Aficionados call this Faubourg Marigny bistro "a well-kept secret" for "haute" Eclectic cuisine and "refreshing mojitos" among a "casually dressed" crowd; both the "chic" room looking out onto Frenchmen Street and the "accommodating" servers set the stage for a "comfortable" meal, and for those who fret it's "not really worth the price tag", Sunday brunch offers more "value" with live jazz tunes by the Pfister Sisters.

Mark Twain's Pizza ⊠Ⓜ   22 11 16 $16
2035 Metairie Rd. (Atherton Dr.), 504-832-8032;
www.marktwainspizza.com
Pizza "beyond the ordinary" with an "outstanding crust and quality ingredients", in versions such as Creole, Hawaiian and a feta-topped 'Mysterious Stranger', attract pie pundits to this Old Metairie strip-mall spot; drawbacks include "what-a-dump" decor, "long lines" and "upsetting hours of operation" (8 PM closing time).

Martinique Bistro Ⓜ   25 | 22 | 22 | $40
5908 Magazine St. (bet. Eleonore & State Sts.),
504-891-8495
Locals wax rhapsodic about the "exquisite" "seasonal" French cuisine with a seafood forte at this "tiny", "intimate" Uptown "sleeper", which opens onto a "transporting" garden patio; the staff is generally "attentive and unobtrusive", and meals run long with "romance" in the air; N.B. chef Nick Wood took over the stove this year.

Martin Wine Cellar   23 | 14 | 16 | $16
714 Elmeer Ave. (Veterans Memorial Blvd.), 504-896-7350;
www.martinwine.com
This Metairie vino depot stocks aisles and aisles of "extraordinary" bottles, but it's the "always-packed" eat-in deli that has locals jockeying for a fix of "fresh", "incredible" "oversized" sandwiches – and of course, "wine with lunch" – at a "price-to-quality ratio that can't be beat"; N.B. the Uptown location was damaged heavily in Katrina and is closed; there are temporary, wine and spirits–only locations Uptown and in Mandeville.

Mat & Naddie's Ⓢ   25 | 22 | 21 | $32
937 Leonidas St. (Freret St.), 504-861-9600
"Never met a dish here I didn't want to take home" says one wag of this "spunky" Carrollton Contemporary Louisiana bistro that "impresses" with "innovative" cooking, and has recently resumed serving dinner Friday, Saturday and Monday in addition to its weekday lunch buffet – a "great value" at $10 ($5 for kids); its "welcoming" staff and "sophisticated" cottage setting, with a patio where you can "watch the sun drop", keep it all the more "popular."

Meauxbar Ⓢ Ⓜ   – | – | – | M
942 N. Rampart St. (St. Philip St.), 504-569-9979
Chef Matthew Guidry and partner Jim Conte left their Sag Harbor restaurant to bring their French bistro cuisine, homemade ice creams and sorbet-kissed Meaux Juleps to a vintage Vieux Carré corner building sporting high ceilings and chic tiled floors; both Quarterites and folks who come over from the Marigny think it's mo' betta for a quiet dinner with friends.

Melting Pot, The NEW   18 | 20 | 20 | $42
1820 St. Charles Ave. (Felicity St.), 504-525-3225;
www.meltingpot.com
Groups and couples alike dip into "delicious" "decadent" fondues (cheese, "boiling meats" or chocolate), at this "comfortable" Lower Garden District newcomer, part of an upscale "Swiss concept" chain; advocates appreciate it simply for the "social", "cook-it-yourself" "experience", but the woeful wonder "who knew hot cheese could cost so much?"

Middendorf's Seafood Ⓜ　　25 14 20 $20

30160 Hwy. 51 S. (I-55, exit 15), Manchac, 985-386-6666
"Wafer-thin", "crispy" catfish is "the bomb" at this
72-year-old seafooder, a "rustic" "regional treasure" so
"down-home and real" that New Orleanians don't hesitate
to drive the 45 minutes to swampy Lake Manchac to get
there; the child-friendly dining room has waitresses
"who've been there since WWII", making it all the more
precious since the loss of the West End's seafood houses.

Mike Serio's Po-Boys & Deli Ⓢ　　18 11 14 $12

133 St. Charles Ave. (bet. Canal & Common Sts.), 504-523-2668
"Locals galore" crowd this "greasy spoon sandwich
shop" for the "fabulous po' boys" ("it's one of the few
places that will make a ham" version) as well as cheap
plate-lunch specials; it's also "LSU fan headquarters" with
Tigers memorabilia covering the walls, so if you're a
Tulane fan, look away.

Mike's on the Avenue Ⓢ Ⓜ　　– – – E

Hotel Le Cirque, 936 St. Charles Ave. (Howard Ave.),
504-962-0900
Former New Orleans chef Mike Fennelly is still in Hawaii,
but his spirit is back and channeling through friend and
recently arrived chef Kate Chadwick, whose menu of
Asian tapas brings together new creations with favorites
from the first Mike's; set inside the Hotel Le Cirque,
the spare, chic dining room and bar overlooks the Lee
Circle streetcar line.

Mimi's Ⓢ Ⓜ　　23 19 22 $29

Mark Twain Shopping Ctr., 10160 Jefferson Hwy.
(bet. Mark Twain Dr. & Sauve Rd.), 504-737-6464
This "secret" Creole-Italian River Ridger reinvented itself
with a more upscale menu after Katrina, adding entrees
such as honey-glazed duck and shrimp Victoria and new
desserts like mocha crème brûlée, which could explain
why the Food score jumped considerably this year;
"speedy", "friendly" service and a "charming" bistro atmosphere laced with jazz make it a natural "when you
want to stay close to home in the 'burbs."

Minnie's Catfish Corner Ⓢ NEW　　– – – I

3735 Ulloa St. (Tulane Ave.), 504-324-8994;
www.minniescatfishcorner.com
Trenchermen's portions of fresh, hot fried catfish, baked
macaroni, red and white beans and fried chicken slide
across the kitchen counter at this soul food haven, a corner spot that's a slight jog off tattered Tulane Avenue in
Central City; bright red walls liven up the space, while a
flat-screen TV normally tuned to sports keeps construction
workers and neighborhood folks content; N.B. closes
at 8 PM.

Miyako
22 | 18 | 21 | $28

1403 St. Charles Ave. (Thalia St.), 504-410-9997
3837 Veterans Memorial Blvd. (Taft Park), 504-779-6475
www.japanesebistro.com
"Kids of all sizes" get a kick out of the "skilled chefs" and their "entertaining" hibachi hijinks at these Lower Garden District and Metairie Japanese spots, which serve "solid sushi" in addition to table-grilled goods; many surveyors say it's "always excellent", particularly for group dinners or a "bargain" lunch, though it can get a little "rushed."

Mona Lisa
20 | 14 | 17 | $19

1212 Royal St. (bet. Barracks & Governor Nicholls Sts.), 504-522-6746
"Excellent eggplant parm" and other Italian eats draw the young and the "value"-conscious to this "soulful" "French Quarter secret"; varied renditions of the eponymous portrait dot the decaying brick walls of the "quirky", "candlelit" room, and its BYO option with a $5 corkage fee (in addition to house bottles) keeps the tab low.

Mona's Cafe
21 | 13 | 18 | $15

3901 Banks St. (S. Scott St.), 504-482-7743
504 Frenchmen St. (Decatur St.), 504-949-4115
4126 Magazine St. (bet. Marengo & Milan Sts.), 504-894-9800
"Fantastic" falafel, "mmm" hummus and killer kebabs are a few of the specialties at this "authentic" Middle Eastern trio where you can BYO or quaff exotic Lebanese iced tea; it provides "service with a smile" and "reasonable prices", though some say it has all "the charm of a cafeteria."

Morning Call Coffee Stand ●⊘⇥
24 | 17 | 19 | $7

Lakeside Plaza, 3325 Severn Ave. (17th St.), 504-885-4068
It's "hard for New Orleanians to admit", but many say the "best" beignets and "classic" chicory café au lait can be found at this Metairie strip-mall spot where almost "everything costs $1.40"; open 24 hours on the weekends, it's prime for "people-watching – even if they're suburbanites."

Morton's, The Steakhouse
24 | 23 | 24 | $61

Shops at Canal Pl., 365 Canal St. (N. Peters St.), 504-566-0221;
www.mortons.com
"Luxe steaks" summon chops chums to this French Quarter link in a national chain; the "great martinis", "clubby" atmosphere and "warm, professional service" help justify the "extreme prices", but for better or worse, "if you've been to one Morton's, then you've been to this one too."

MOSCA'S ⊠Ⓜ⇥
27 | 12 | 20 | $38

4137 Hwy. 90 W. (bet. Butler Dr. & Live Oak Blvd.), Avondale, 504-436-9942
"I'd do dishes to eat here!" exclaim enthusiasts about this hallowed "old roadhouse" in Avondale, which plates up a

"garlic-powered" Italian menu of "authentic", "inspired" creations like chicken à la grande and oysters Mosca, served "family-style" to a crowd that always includes a few fascinating "characters"; insiders advise "call first to get directions", "bring at least six people so you can get everything on the menu" and "take cash."

MOTHER'S ⊠   24 | 9 | 13 | $15 |

401 Poydras St. (bet. Magazine & Tchoupitoulas Sts.), 504-523-9656; www.mothersrestaurant.net
"It would be a sin" to miss this ever-crowded CBD Cajun-American "cafeteria-style" "dive", a destination for "down-home" vittles like the 'debris' po-boy ("a thing of dripping beauty"), "out-of-this-world" étouffée and the "best damn ham", along with "hangover-curing" breakfasts; "tourist-trap" prices and "lines out the door" are drawbacks, but at least the "surly service" adds "character."

Mr. Ed's ⊠   22 | 17 | 20 | $21 |

1001 Live Oak St. (bet. Bonnabel Blvd. & Lake Ave.), 504-838-0022
Devotees "don't want the secret out" about the "very, very good" Creole "comfort food" (fried chicken, po' boys, bread pudding) and Italian dishes at this Metairie hideaway; its "homestyle" brand of "fried everything" is a magnet for thrifty "senior citizens" and other "neighborhood" noshers, half of whom "seem to know Ed" himself.

Mr. Gyros   ▽ 21 | 11 | 18 | $16 |

3620 N. Causeway Blvd. (W. Esplanade Ave.), 504-833-9228; www.mrgyrosmetairie.com
Appealing gyros, among other "good Greek basics", distinguish this spartan locale near the Lakeside Mall; regulars assure it's "where Greeks in the city go to eat", and makes for a "quick" and "affordable" shopping break besides – just watch out for a "crowded" lunch scene.

Mr. John's Ristorante ⊠ Ⓜ   ▽ 26 | 18 | 22 | $45 |

2111 St. Charles Ave. (bet. Jackson Ave. & Josephine St.), 504-679-7697; www.mrjohnssteakhouse.com
While beef eaters who've discovered this "real sleeper" in the Lower Garden District declare its choice cuts "shouldn't be a secret", many find the "superb Italian specialties" added to its post-Katrina menu just as "exciting"; its "friendly service", sidewalk seating and "views of St. Charles Avenue" are just gravy.

Mulate's of New Orleans   17 | 16 | 15 | $27 |

201 Julia St. (Convention Center Blvd.), 504-522-1492; www.mulates.com
"Go for the music and have a few beers" recommend visitors to this Warehouse District ragin' Cajun, a "conventioneer's best friend" where dancing to live Acadian bands makes for a "noisy" "NOLA experience"; the food itself, "heaping platters" of "fried everything" along with black-

ened alligator and red beans and rice, stirs up a gumbo of reviews ranging from "damn tasty" to "don't bother."

MURIEL'S JACKSON SQUARE 23 26 22 $42
Jackson Sq., 801 Chartres St. (St. Ann St.), 504-568-1885;
www.muriels.com
"Imaginatively decorated" rooms "ranging from haunting to haunted" beguile guests (and a few "resident ghosts") at this "festive", "romantic" Creole "overlooking Jackson Square"; from its "rich and tasty creations" at a "fair price" to its "smiling service" and "historic charm" – particularly in the "decadent" Seance Lounge where you "feel like a sultan" – it's "what the French Quarter is all about"; N.B. the Food rating may not reflect a recent chef change.

Nacho Mama's 13 12 14 $16
3242 Magazine St. (Pleasant St.), 504-899-0031;
www.nachomamasneworleans.com
3808 Veterans Blvd. (N. Turnbull Dr.), 504-780-7804 ⊠
"Heaping high" plates of tacos, nachos and other Mexican dishes attract student and business crowds to this Metairie and Uptown duo for a fajita fix or round of "strong margaritas"; while it's "casual" and "easy on the budget", its Food score has dipped since the last *Survey,* and many shrug "don't go out of your way" for these "passable" places.

Napoleon House 19 24 17 $21
500 Chartres St. (St. Louis St.), 504-524-9752;
www.napoleonhouse.com
"May it never close" say worshipers of this "classic", "moody" French Quarter "hangout" built in 1797, whose "crumbling" "interior oozes character"; while Creole-Med dishes like jambalaya and warm muffalettas satisfy, it's "all about the atmosphere" and savoring a "wonderful" Pimm's Cup, "classical music" and "blissful" courtyard – just don't be put-off by the traditionally "grumpy", "bow-tied waiters"; P.S. "menu and hours are limited post-Katrina."

Nardo's Trattoria ⊠ Ⓜ 18 15 19 $32
6078 Laurel St. (Webster St.), 504-895-9441;
www.nardostrattoria.com
The "mindful staff" "tries hard" at this "earnest" Northern Italian, an upmarket Uptowner in a renovated tavern, which serves "respectable" fare and "reasonably priced superTuscans"; some compliment the "attractive" interior, which sports the original copper-topped bar, though others think it lends "fancy" airs to what's simply "mamma's cooking."

New Orleans Food & Spirits ⊠ 25 15 19 $20
208 Lee Ln. (bet. E. Boston & E. Rutland Sts.), Covington,
985-875-0432
2330 Lapalco Blvd. (Brooklyn Ave.), Harvey, 504-362-0800
If it gets "noisy" at these counter-service Cajuns in Covington and Harvey, that's because "everything on the

menu screams 'good eating!'", including the house specialty — "fabulous", "hangin' off the plate" fried seafood that's "fresh", "lightly battered" and dished out in "huge portions"; since they're both so "popular", "be prepared to wait at least 30 minutes."

NEW ORLEANS GRILL   24 | 28 | 25 | $63

Windsor Court Hotel, 300 Gravier St. (bet. S. Peters & Tchoupitoulas Sts.), 504-522-1992; www.windsorcourthotel.com
The "world-class" dining room, embellished with plush banquettes and floral arrangements among other "formal, elegant" touches, is the calling card of this "posh" Windsor Court Hotel destination, voted No. 1 in the *Survey* for Decor; though some sniff that "stuffy is an understatement" for the ambiance, most recommend this CBD "classic" for "a special night out with all the trimmings" — so "dress up" and prepare to feel (and spend) "like royalty"; N.B. new chef Michael Collins' internationally influenced New American menu may outdate the Food score.

New Orleans   17 | 12 | 14 | $13
Hamburger & Seafood Co.
817 Veterans Memorial Blvd. (Martin Berhman Ave.), 504-837-8580
6920 Veterans Memorial Blvd. (David Dr.), 504-455-1272
www.nohsc.com
"A notch above fast food", this local chainlet in Metairie offers an "extensive menu" of "surprisingly good" burgers, po' boys and Creole seafood that can be spiced up at the "amazing fixin's bar"; though it's not fancy, supporters say it gives "everybody in your party something they want" in "quick", "inexpensive" and "family-friendly" style.

New York Pizza   21 | 8 | 15 | $14
5201 Magazine St. (Dufosset St.), 504-891-2376
"Hot", "crispy" "New York–style" thin-crust pizza prepared with "different sauces" and toppings have customers praising the pies at this Uptown joint; many say "eating in is not a real treat" due to charm-free premises and service with "attitude", so they "just get a pizza and get out fast."

Nine Roses   25 | 15 | 17 | $20
1100 Stephens St. (Westbank Expwy.), 504-366-7665
Both "adventurous" newcomers and longtime pho fans savor the "brilliant Vietnamese" dishes served at this "authentic" West Bank family spot; since the menu is "phone book"–sized, the portions "generous" and the prices gentle, it's an "excellent place to get people together and use the lazy Susan."

NINJA Ⓜ   23 | 15 | 19 | $23
8433 Oak St. (S. Carrollton Ave.), 504-866-1119
"Creative", "always fresh" raw fish "rocks" the regulars at this Carrollton Japanese where the staff is "pleasant" and

the "sushi clock performs on the hour"; nevertheless, both the "sterile" space and the "smelly", "dank basement bar you must go through to get there" are off-putting to some.

Nirvana Indian Cuisine Ⓜ   20 17 17 $21
4308 Magazine St. (Napoleon Ave.), 504-894-9797;
www.insidenirvana.com
"Let's face it, New Orleans doesn't really have much in terms of Indian food", but when you "crave the burn", this Uptowner appeases with "better-than-average" versions of standard subcontinental dishes that also make "great takeout"; a "pleasant atmosphere" prevails despite uneven service, but alas, the price of the "killer" lunch buffet has climbed since Katrina.

NOLA   26 23 24 $51
534 St. Louis St. (bet. Chartres & Decatur Sts.), 504-522-6652;
www.emerils.com
"Delicious Creole-inspired" Contemporary Louisiana cuisine "served with style" draws the masses to Emeril's "alternative" French Quarter outpost, which many find "hipper" and "more casual" than his namesake venue; most agree it's a "good value" for the price and "runs like a clock", though the "touristy" crowd ups the "noise to stratospheric levels."

Nuvolari's   23 23 22 $45
246 Gerard St. (Jefferson St.), Mandeville, 985-626-5619;
www.nuvolaris.com
This "backbone of Old Mandeville dining" serves a "consistent" menu of "excellent" Italian fare with a focus on "fresh seafood"; its evocative old building, "dark woods" and gracious lighting make it a "warm" place to "relax" with cocktails after work, or splurge on dinner "for a first date."

Oak Alley Restaurant   - - - I
Oak Alley Plantation, 3645 Hwy. 18 (3 mi. west of Hwy. 20),
Vacherie, 225-265-2151; www.oakalleyplantation.com
"If you feel like going somewhere" outside the city, the majestic 1836 River Road plantation housing this Cajun-Creole cottage "in the shadows of stately oaks" commands attention; but opinions are mixed on the restaurant itself, which, although staffed by "nice servers", offers fare that some call "skillfully" prepared and others find "lacking in flavor"; N.B. breakfast and lunch only.

O'Henry's Food & Spirits   13 12 13 $16
301 Baronne St. (Gravier St.), 504-522-5242 ✉
634 S. Carrollton Ave. (Hampson St.), 504-866-9741 ☽
710 Terry Pkwy. (Carol Sue Ave.), 504-433-4111
8859 Veterans Blvd. (bet. Massachusetts & Mississippi Aves.),
504-461-9840 ☽
www.ohenrys.com
Those with "a real love" for "throwing peanut shells on the floor" will appreciate this Traditional American mini-chain, a

"no-fuss" "children's favorite" and college hangout that's big on "ok burgers" and fries at "bargain" prices, with the bonus of an "outside balcony" at the Riverbend location; but the dissatisfied say they'd opt for "ballpark food" instead.

Olivier's　　　　　　　　24 | 21 | 22 | $45
204 Decatur St. (bet. Bienville Ave. & Iberville St.), 504-525-7734; www.olivierscreole.com
"Grandma's recipe" Creole cooking, including "fantastic" signature rabbit and "the best peach cobbler in NOLA", have enthusiasts chatting up this French Quarter "find" ("your biggest challenge is to figure out what you don't want to order"); the setting's "comfortable", with "timely", "personable" service and "warm greetings" from owner Armand Olivier, "one cool Creole cat."

One Restaurant ⊠　　　　　24 | 21 | 23 | $38
8132 Hampson St. (bet. Carrollton Ave. & Dublin St.), 504-301-9061; www.one-sl.com
"Mouthwatering" is the word on this "modern" singular sensation in the Riverbend, where chef Scott Snodgrass (ex Clancy's) creates "unique", "eclectic" New American dishes; the "stylish" room, complete with an open kitchen, is subject to high noise levels, with diners seated "so close you could eat off each others' plates", but the relatively "affordable" tab helps take the edge off.

Oscar's　　　　　　▽ 19 | 12 | 15 | $16
2027 Metairie Rd. (Jefferson Ave.), 504-831-9540
This 21-and-over American "joint" in Old Metairie hits the spot with "great giant hamburgers", "stuffed baked potatoes" and other "simple, straightforward" bar fare; among its trappings are a dartboard, pool tables and walls of Marilyn Monroe memorabilia, which lend it the dingy glamour of a "perfect hideout."

Palace Café Ⓜ　　　　　24 | 24 | 23 | $40
605 Canal St. (Chartres St.), 504-523-1661; www.palacecafe.com
That "Brennan family spit-and-polish" is alive and well at Dickie Brennan's "fabulous and fancy" nouvelle Creole where "classic New Orleans cuisine" with a twist ("to-die-for" crabmeat cheesecake, "exceptional" white chocolate bread pudding) is served by an "above-par" staff; French Quarter businesspeople and tourists swarm at lunch, but locals love the "sleeper" Sunday brunch, "a wonderful way" to wake up with live jazz and "sunlight gleaming through the large windows."

P&G ⊠　　　　　　▽ 15 | 3 | 9 | $11
345 Baronne St. (Union St.), 504-525-9678
"Fried is their favorite food group" at this cafeterialike "greasy spoon", which caters to CBD crowds with "decent" "blue-plate lunches" and "fried seafood po' boys to keep you weighed down all day"; it's "crazy at lunchtime"

with a "Soup Nazi vibe to the service" and "no clearly de-
fined line", so "just jump in and order."

Parasol's   23 | 12 | 17 | $13
2533 Constance St. (3rd St.), 504-899-2054;
www.parasols.com
"The only thing thicker than the gravy is the atmosphere"
at this 55-year-old Garden District Irish bar/sandwich
shop/fry house, a "local" "destination for roast beef po'
boys" "so messy and delicious you'll be licking your el-
bows"; partiers say "don't miss the St. Paddy's day celebration", when the green beer flows into the street from
this "tiny", "dilapidated" shrine.

Parkway Bakery Ⓜ   25 | 16 | 18 | $11
538 Hagan Ave. (Moss St.), 504-482-3047
Neighbors and nostalgia buffs moon over this old-timer
overlooking Bayou St. John, a Mid-City "po' boy heaven"
dishing up the "definitive" roast beef sandwich, "dripping
with gravy" and served with "Barq's longnecks"; an "outpost of civilization during the recovery", it boasts plenty of
"nostalgic mementos on the walls", and with live music on
the weekends, life just "doesn't get any better."

Pascal's Manale Ⓢ   23 | 18 | 21 | $36
1838 Napoleon Ave. (Barrone St.), 504-895-4877
"Don the bib" at this "old-line" Uptown New Orleans–style
Italian and dig into the "one thing to order here" – "best-in-
the-world", "melt-in-your-mouth" BBQ shrimp in all their
"messy" glory; bivalve boosters believe the oyster bar is
"where it's at", while others take comfort in the celeb
photo–bedecked dining room; either way, all cheer on this
"old-school" place as it "makes a comeback."

Pelican Club Ⓢ Ⓜ   26 | 24 | 23 | $48
312 Exchange Pl. (Bienville St.), 504-523-1504;
www.pelicanclub.com
"Cozy, clubby" and "off the beaten path in the French
Quarter", this "upscale" New American set in a 19th-century
townhouse is "well worth seeking out" for "wonderful
meals" with a seafood emphasis; regulars recommend
"dressing up", bringing a "large group" and starting off with
a cocktail at the "great bar with live piano" on the weekends.

PERISTYLE Ⓢ Ⓜ   26 | 24 | 24 | $55
1041 Dumaine St. (Burgundy St.), 504-593-9535
Most style mavens agree that chef-owner Tom Wolfe does
this French Quarter mecca "proud" by serving "refreshing", "well-realized" French–Contemporary Louisiana fare
that boasts an "innovative melding of flavors"; yes, some
still "miss Anne Kearney", the former chef/co-owner, but
as consolation, the "long-term staff" is "attentive" "without being pretentious", complementing the "historic"
"charm" of this "teeny bistro with big food."

Petunia's   24 20 22 $24
817 St. Louis St. (Bourbon St.), 504-522-6440;
www.petuniasrestaurant.com
"Go hungry" for the "amazing" breakfast at this "quaint"
Cajun-Creole in a pink 19th-century French Quarter house,
where "huge, scrumptious crêpes" and three-egg omelets
(so big they're "either made with ostrich eggs or the chef
can't count") are "worth every gut-busting bite"; a
"cheery" interior and "flamboyant" service make dining
here a hoot; N.B. open for dinner Thursday to Sunday.

P.F. Chang's China Bistro Ⓜ   22 21 19 $25
Lakeside Mall, 3301 Veterans Memorial Blvd.
(N. Causeway Blvd.), 504-828-5288; www.pfchangs.com
"Yeah, it's a chain; yeah, it's pricey for Chinese – I still love it"
sums up the sentiment surrounding the Metairie branch of
this "franchise operation" with a "hip Asian vibe" and design; among the "Americanized" but "consistently good"
eats, "the lettuce wraps are a must", and the "staff teaches
you how to order and mix" everything else (though a few
folks "feel they're being rushed out" by such ministrations).

Pho Bang   ▽ 23 8 15 $14
14367 Chef Menteur Hwy. (Alcee Fortier Blvd.), 504-254-3929
1028 Manhattan Blvd. (Westbank Expwy.), 504-365-0339 ⊅
"When the local Vietnamese frequent an establishment, it's
the real deal" say fans of the pho and "light and fresh" spring
rolls at these "five-star" spots with no-star prices in Harvey
and New Orleans East; though their looks and locations don't
entice, most find them "worth the drive" nonetheless.

Pho Tau Bay   25 11 18 $14
Expressway Bowling Lanes Shopping Ctr.,
113C Westbank Expwy. (Lafayette St.), 504-368-9846
"Big bowls of soup with a whole lot going on in them",
among other "excellent" Vietnamese dishes, warm up
guests to this "wonderful", "refreshing" West Bank "favorite" where you "eat like royalty" but pony up "like students";
with these assets, no one complains about the "antiquated
strip-mall" setting that "doesn't look like much."

PJ's Coffee & Tea Co.   19 14 17 $7
7624 Maple St. (Hillary St.), 504-866-7031
800 Metairie Rd. (Focis St.), 504-828-1460
Tulane University, 24 McAlister Dr. (Freret St.), 504-865-5705
4480 Hwy. 22 (Moores Rd.), Mandeville, 985-624-9015
www.pjscoffee.com
Undergrads and locals suck down "deep, rich coffee" that
"beats Starbucks by a mile" at these "comfy", "down-to-
earth" branches of a "NOLA-friendly" Southern chain; on a
steamy morn, "fabulous granitas" and iced coffees can be
seen in almost every hand, along with pastries ranging
from "fresh" to "mediocre"; alas, it's "hit-or-miss" service.

Popeyes
22 | 7 | 7 | $9

3825 General de Gaulle Dr. (Holiday Dr.), 504-362-6033
4041 Magazine St. (Marengo St.), 504-895-8608
4238 S. Claiborne Ave. (Napoleon Ave.), 504-269-8171
1243 St. Charles Ave. (bet. Clio & Erato Sts.), 504-522-1362
www.popeyes.com
New Orleans' "fast-food icon", this "cheap" homegrown
chain serves up the "best fried chicken anywhere" according to fans of crunchy, "spicy and delicious" birds
served with "indulgent" sides like buttery biscuits and
dirty rice; the no-frills service and decor make it "good for
a quick take-out meal" on days when you'd rather "feel
your arteries harden" at home.

Port of Call ●
24 | 13 | 14 | $17

838 Esplanade Ave. (Dauphine St.), 504-523-0120;
www.portofcallneworleans.com
"Bountiful" "burgers so good you'd think they invented
them", "mammoth baked potatoes" and "powerful"
Monsoon cocktails (they'll "throw you for a loop") are the
siren song of this "dark", "divey" French Quarter bar; despite the scruffy "nautical decor" and "slow-as-molasses
bartenders", it's a "New Orleans institution", "always
packed" with salty locals.

Praline Connection
21 | 14 | 18 | $21

542 Frenchmen St. (Chartres St.), 504-943-3934;
www.pralineconnection.com
This "relaxed" Marigny soul food spot (serving "much
more than just pralines") dishes up "homestyle Southern"
food, from "smothered chicken and greens" to fried okra;
the black-and-white decor is "not flashy", "service can be
a little slow" (though "cheery") and some say the cooking
has its "off nights" – but the majority respects that it's "not
too dumbed-down for the tourist trade."

Pupuseria La Macarena Ⓜ ⊅
∇ 18 | 6 | 17 | $13

4221 Williams Blvd. (42nd St.), 504-464-4525
Formerly a "microscopic" West Bank cult fave, this casual, family-run Pan-Latin is now purveying pupusas (meat
or cheese pan-fried tortillas) and other Salvadoran specialties in roomier digs to the Kenner crowd; a few foes
find it "overpriced for what it is."

Raising Cane's
17 | 12 | 14 | $8

4036 Veterans Memorial Blvd. (bet. Lake Villa Dr. &
Richland Ave.), 504-297-1632; www.raisingcanes.com
If you want "cooked-in-yo-mama's-kitchen" chicken fin-
gers served with a "creamy", "kick-booty sauce" ("their
secret weapon"), head for this fast-food chain link with
"insanely perky service"; just keep in mind "they do only
one thing" (plus a few sides), and some can't understand
"what all the crowing's about."

RALPH'S ON THE PARK ⓜ   24   27   24 $43
900 City Park Ave. (N. Alexander St.), 504-488-1000;
www.ralphsonthepark.com
Ralph Brennan's "beautiful" renovation of an 1860 building
"overlooking City Park's magnificent oaks" wins the highest praise for its "sweeping vista", "stunning dining room"
and "swinging bar"; most agree that the French-accented
Contemporary Louisiana cuisine served by an "accommodating staff" "lives up to the Brennan tradition", and the location makes it "perfect" for ladies who lunch before
visiting the nearby "sculpture garden at NOMA."

R & O's ⓜ   23   11   18 $18
216 Hammond Hwy. (Lake Ave.), 504-831-1248
"Don't dress up" – just "bring your crying baby" along with
the "whole family" to this "noisy" "authentic" Bucktown
"dive" for "delicious grub", including "gravy-soaked" po'
boys and "great" fried seafood, along with pizza and other
Italian eats; the "fast service" is spoken "in Yat – as in,
'where ya't, dawlin?'", elevating "local flavor" to an art form.

Red Fish Grill   22   20   21 $34
115 Bourbon St. (Canal St.), 504-598-1200; www.redfishgrill.com
Tourists and "fiercely loyal foodies" are bedfellows at
Ralph Brennan's "bustling", "comfortable" Bourbon Street
fish house where "awesome" "fresh" seafood and "wonderful" chocolate bread pudding come in "generous portions" at "moderate prices"; the "open" dining room with its
"industrial" aquatic look adds festivity – but go elsewhere
for a tête-à-tête as it's "noisier than a flock of seagulls" too.

Reginelli's Pizzeria   20   15   16 $16
Citrus Palm Shopping Ctr., 5608 Citrus Blvd. (Elmwood Park Blvd.),
504-818-0111
3244 Magazine St. (Pleasant St.), 505-895-7272
741 State St. (bet. Constance & Magazine Sts.), 504-899-1414
817 W. Esplanade Ave. (Bourbon St.), 504-712-6868
www.reginellis.com
"Terrific" upper-crust but "reasonably priced" pizza is the
ticket at this "relaxed", "hip" local chainlet, which also
serves salads and other "creative" combos ("love the as-
paragus panini") to students, families and "as many kids
as Chuck E. Cheese"; still, a few complain of "inconsis-
tent" cooking – "sometimes sandwiches are bare of ingredients and other times, they're delicious."

Remoulade   20   16   17 $23
309 Bourbon St. (Bienville Ave.), 504-523-0377;
www.remoulade.com
"All the great Creole foods of the city, from muffalettas to po'
boys" are on offer at this "casual arm of Arnaud's" around
the corner; it's "less expensive" and "more relaxed" than
its brother, but boasts, some say, the same "excellent"

fare ("hello, it's cooked in Arnaud's kitchen"); however, skeptics slam the "super-touristy" Bourbon Street site as "no big deal", especially given the "mediocre" service.

RESTAURANT DES FAMILLES ⓜ | 24 | 27 | 24 | $27 |
7163 Barataria Blvd. (Lafitte Pkwy.), 504-689-7834
"If you want fresh seafood, go to the swamp" – or rather, to this "serene" restaurant that "sits on the Bayou des Familles", "surrounded by cypress trees", with an "antebellum plantation ambiance"; "nice people" serve "absolutely lovely" Cajun surf 'n' turf classics ("gumbo like my Cajun grandmother made"), and while it's "a long way out, it's worth it" "if you can get seated at a table along the windows" ("you may even see an alligator or heron").

Rib Room | 25 | 25 | 25 | $50 |
Omni Royal Orleans, 621 St. Louis St. (Chartres St.), 504-529-7046;
www.omnihotels.com
"A great place for beef in a seafood town", this "sophisticated" steakhouse is a "longtime favorite of French Quarter residents" thanks to its "famous prime rib" among other cuts; a "power-lunch" scene, warm "hospitality" and window seats for "watching people walk by" on Royal Street add to the allure, though opinions differ as to whether the polished new look is "reinvigorating" or has turned a "one-of-a-kind place" into a typical "nice hotel restaurant."

Riccobono's Peppermill ⓜ | 21 | 19 | 21 | $21 |
(aka Peppermill)
3524 Severn Ave. (12th St.), 504-455-2266
"Consistently good for over 30 years", this family-run, casual old shoe in Metairie attracts a clientele that's "young at heart, [if] not in years"; the "country Italian"-Creole cooking comes "at reasonable prices" at every meal, but the "wonderful full-service breakfast" is the main event, complete with droll, motherly waitresses ("was told to finish my eggs before she'd refill my coffee!").

Riche ⓢ ⓜ NEW | – | – | – | E |
Harrah's Hotel, 228 Poydras St. (Fulton St.), 504-533-6117
This posh new CBD lair is celebrity chef Todd English's 12th venture in his nationwide restaurant empire as well as his first French foray – an interpretation of a classic brasserie serving dishes like garlic soup, *frisée aux lardons* and steak frites, complemented by a vast yet nuanced wine list; amid the red damask draperies and faux marble walls, high rollers and haute cuisine–seekers are served by a brisk staff, who provide able guidance for the uninitiated.

RioMar ⓢ | 25 | 19 | 21 | $37 |
800 S. Peters St. (Julia St.), 504-525-3474;
www.riomarseafood.com
"Ceviche rules the menu" at this Warehouse District fintasia serving "inventive", "fresh seafood" prepared with

"Spanish and Latin American flair" by "serious chef" Adolfo Garcia; the "moderately priced wines", "boisterous" atmosphere and "thoughtful", "efficient" service also impress, and even fish-phobes can't complain since "everyone looks beautiful after a couple of sangrias."

Ristorante Da Piero ⓈⓂ   ▽ 27 | 23 | 27 | $42

401 Williams Blvd. (4th St.), 504-469-8585;
www.ristorantedapiero.net

Regulars rave about the "authentic" Emilian fare at this traditionally styled, "family-run" "find" in Kenner, whose "fabulous homemade pastas" and "simple but creative" seafood dishes are matched by an "excellent" Italian wine list; an opera singer performing Tuesdays and Thursdays, plus live jazz on the weekends, make it a feast for the ears as well.

Ristorante Filippo Ⓢ   ▽ 22 | 20 | 21 | $34

1917 Ridgelake Dr. (38th St.), 504-835-4008

A "mouthwatering" menu with such signatures as veal parmesan and calamari make fans of this "friendly" Metairie Italian moan "mamma mia!" with delight; it's a "comfortable" "hole-in-the-wall, out of an old black-and-white movie", with the added benefit of being "remarkably inexpensive" to boot.

Rock-n-Sake Bar & Sushi Ⓜ   24 | 19 | 20 | $28

823 Fulton St. (bet. Julia & St. Joseph Sts.), 504-581-7253;
www.rocknsake.com

"Not your typical sushi place", this Warehouse District Japanese draws raves for its "amazingly fresh", amusingly named "creative" fare ("Hawaii-5-0 roll", "orgasm roll") served amid the urban-chic environs of "really cool" decor and "loud techno" beats (please "turn down the music so my waiter can hear what I'm ordering"); if you stay late, expect a "crazed scene" with "many Paris Hilton look-alikes."

Roly Poly   17 | 9 | 15 | $9

One Shell Sq., 701 Poydras Sq., 504-561-9800 Ⓢ
5409 Tchoupitoulas St. (Jefferson Ave.), 504-891-8373
www.rolypoly.com

"Wrap and roll, baby" say those in the swing of this lunch-friendly pair Uptown and in the CBD, whose sandwich wraps are "inventive" and "healthy too, if that's your thing"; but some surveyors scold that the staff moves "at the speed of molasses", "there aren't many places to sit" and "their roly polys should be called flatty wattys" ("give me more meat!").

Royal Blend Coffee & Tea   18 | 17 | 16 | $11

204 Metairie Rd. (Friedrichs Ave.), 504-835-7779
621 Royal St. (Toulouse St.), 504-523-2716
www.royalblendcoffee.com

Visiting this duo of "dressed-up" coffeehouses is "a daily ritual" for reviewers who revel in the "great muffins" and "huge variety of teas" and java ("daily lunch specials" and "tasty" sandwiches are also on hand); the Metairie branch is slightly larger, but the French Quarter location has a "traditional" courtyard with fountain, making it a "tranquil" stop for the foot-weary.

Royal China   25 | 12 | 17 | $21
600 Veterans Memorial Blvd. (Aris Ave.), 504-831-9633
Surveyors stake a bold claim for this Metairie old-timer, saying it serves "the best Chinese food in the New Orleans area" – "large portions of high-quality, freshly prepared" dishes, particularly the "great dim sum", that offer "a feast both for the tongue and the eyes"; however, the price for enjoying the royal treats includes dealing with "gruff" service and decor that "definitely needs attention."

rue de la course ●⧧   16 | 18 | 14 | $8
3121 Magazine St. (9th St.), 504-899-0242
1140 S. Carrollton Ave. (bet. Oak & Zimpel Sts.), 504-861-4343
Known for its "funky" "library-type" air that "national chains wish they could emulate", this "quintessential New Orleans" coffeehouse has two locations: the Carrollton branch is in a "gorgeous" "old bank building", while the Garden District venue has more outdoor seats and a spacious feel; both attract "boho youths" who go for the "excellent strong coffee" and "great pastries", even if the other eats "leave something to be desired" and the staff acts "even cooler than the customers."

Russell's Marina Grill   19 | 15 | 19 | $17
8555 Pontchartrain Blvd. (Lake Marina Ave.), 504-282-9999
A "surprisingly good breakfast joint", this Lakefront American draws early birds and afternoon ham-and-egg hounds for its big plates and "sassy" service in a "Mel's Diner"–like setting, whose "old-time stools and booths" easily accommodate "hungry grandchildren."

Russell's Short Stop Po-Boys ⊠   22 | 7 | 13 | $9
119 Transcontinental Dr. (Thrush St.), 504-885-4572
"Don't let the long lines get you down" – "they move fast" at this Metairie deli serving "one of the best" "overstuffed" roast beef po' boys and "amazing gumbo"; it's a "good-value" neighborhood "staple" for sure, though the peckish "wish they were open longer" (the kitchen closes at 7:30 PM most nights, 9 PM Friday–Saturday).

Ruth's Chris Steak House   25 | 21 | 24 | $54
3633 Veterans Memorial Blvd. (Hessmer Ave.), 504-888-3600;
www.ruthschris.com
This "gold standard" of steakhouse chains still delivers "excellent", "fork-tender" beef at its "clubby" Metairie location, which also maintains "top-level service"; despite steady scores, however, it suffers some unkind cuts from "angry" respondents who complain the "pricey" place has

"lost its local heritage and charm" "since they pulled the corporate HQ out of NOLA" post-Katrina, and did not re-open the Broad Street flagship.

Sake Cafe   23 | 24 | 19 | $28
Independence Mall, 4201 Veterans Memorial Blvd. (bet. Independence St. & Lake Villa Dr.), 504-779-7253
2830 Magazine St. (bet. 6th & Washington Ave.), 504-894-0033; www.sakecafeuptown.com
817 W. Esplanade Ave. (Chateau Blvd.), 504-468-8829
Crescent City sushi seekers say "nothing compares" to this "imaginative" Japanese trio, which "makes a mean roll" as well as "neo-Nippon appetizers" and "innovative fusion dishes", plus cocktails by "great mixologists"; the trend-conscious favor the "modern, sleek" Garden District locale in a renovated K&B drugstore, though some cite "spotty" service overall.

Sal & Judy's Ⓜ   26 | 21 | 22 | $33
27491 Hwy. 190 (14th St.), Lacombe, 985-882-9443
Loyal locals ooh and ahh over the "superb" "Creole-influenced Southern Italian fare" served in "plentiful" portions at this "outstanding" "perennial favorite" in Lacombe; though some say the service falls short of the food, you "can't beat the price" – or path to the top of the waiting list, so "call a week or two ahead" to reserve.

Saltwater Grill Ⓢ   14 | 12 | 13 | $20
1340 S. Carrollton Ave. (bet. Plum & Willow Sts.), 504-324-6640
"In a city known for frying everything", the option of grilled fish in addition to "old-style" sizzled eats and "huge po' boys" helps distinguish the menu at this "basic" Carrollton seafooder; otherwise, "disappointed" diners say it "misses the mark", dishing out "mediocre" food and "indifferent service" that are "not up to the prices."

Sara's ⓈⓂ   22 | 20 | 21 | $28
724 Dublin St. (bet. Hampson & Maple Sts.), 504-861-0565; www.sarasrestaurant.com
"Louisiana meets India", Thailand and the Mediterranean at this "irresistible" Creole-Asian fusion "surprise" serving a "unique", "spicy" menu in Riverbend; both "quirky" and "romantic", the "comfy", couch-strewn spot has a "charming" staff and keeps tabs low with "inexpensive" wines by the glass.

Savvy Gourmet   22 | 22 | 18 | $18
4519 Magazine St. (Jena St.), 504-895-2665; www.savvygourmet.com
Offering a "small" but "scrumptious" New American lunch and brunch menu, this "ultracool" "concept" spot Uptown, which encompasses a cafe, cooking school and kitchenware shop, prepares salads, sandwiches and "wonderful

daily specials" using "locally grown" ingredients; as a "clinic for foodies" that's both "hip" and "kid-friendly", it's become a "gathering place" for culinary shindigs.

Schiro's ∅ ▽ 12 | 12 | 10 | $14

2483 Royal St. (St. Roch Ave.), 504-945-4425;
www.schiroscafe.com

"Large portions" of "down-home food" can be had at this "funky" Bywater "joint" – a Laundromat, grocery store, guest house and restaurant all rolled into one; but many feel the fare "has taken a turn for the worse" since it switched from Med to Cajun-Creole post-Katrina and service is only "hit-or-miss", making it "ok if you're hungry in the neighborhood."

Semolina International Pasta 18 | 17 | 16 | $20

Clearview Mall, 4436 Veterans Memorial Blvd. (Clearview Pkwy.),
504-454-7930
5080 Pontchartrain Blvd. (Metairie Rd.), 504-486-5581
Tyler Square Shopping Ctr., 100 S. Tyler Sq. (21st Ave.), Covington,
985-898-0004
1121 Manhattan Blvd. (bet. Apache & Ute Drs.), Harvey,
504-361-8293
2999 Hwy. 190 (St. Ann Dr.), Mandeville, 985-626-8923
www.semolina.com

This "family-friendly" chain does for pasta what "IHOP did for pancakes", dishing out generous servings of "solid, and sometimes inventive", Italian-Eclectic dishes (chicken enchilada penne, anyone?); skeptics sneer it's "just a step above fast food", but that's what makes it "great for takeout."

Semolina's Bistro Italia – | – | – | M

3226 Magazine St. (Pleasant St.), 504-895-4260;
www.semolina.com

A glamorous dining room with sculptural chairs, old brick walls painted glossy black and a metallic gold ceiling create upscale ambiance at this appealing *nuovo* Italian in the Garden District, a transformation of the former Semolina pasta emporium by the same local chain owners in partnership with Zea; the menu now includes authentic minestrone and lasagna as well as updated fish, chicken and veal dishes, plus its parent kitchen's most popular noodles.

Serrano's Salsa Co. 18 | 18 | 16 | $20

Clearview Mall, 4436 Veterans Memorial Blvd.
(Clearview Pkwy.), 504-780-2354;
www.serranossalsacompany.com

Free salsa and "tasty" queso dip have Metairie honchos "hogging the chips" at this colorful Nuevo Latino in the Clearview Mall; although dishes come in "large portions" and margaritas are made from over 40 brands of tequila, critics cavil "the whole experience still screams chain restaurant" – and a "too expensive" one to boot.

7 on Fulton NEW　　　　24　20　19　$46
Riverfront Hotel, 701 Convention Center Blvd. (Girod St.),
504-681-1034; www.7onfulton.com
Restaurateur Vicky Bayley (Artesia, Ohi'a) "does it
again", presenting "standout", "creative" Contemporary
Louisiana cuisine in the Warehouse District; while some
find the room "beautiful", like something out of "sophisticated LA" (the city, that is), others cite a "hotel atmosphere" and "sluggish service" in need of improvement to
match the price; N.B. the recent arrival of chef Michael
Sichel (ex The Cellar, now closed) may not be reflected by
the Food score.

Shogun Japanese　　　　26　17　20　$29
2325 Veterans Memorial Blvd. (Metairie Ct.),
504-833-7477
Sushi lovers dine swimmingly at this 25-year-old Metairie
mainstay that serves some of the "freshest" "highest
quality" raw fish in town, and entertains with tableside
hibachi cooking performed by "talented" "artist/chefs";
though "minor language barriers" can arise and the
space is less than luxuriant, it's "family-friendly" and
"almost always crowded."

Shula's NEW　　　　20　22　21　$70
JW Marriott, 614 Canal St. (Camp St.), 504-525-6500;
www.donshula.com
A twofer of "tasty" steaks with a nostalgic side of football
touches down at this white-tablecloth sirloin and seafood
house – part of the chain owned by former NFL coach Don
Shula – in the CBD's Marriott hotel; while fans find it a
"nice respite from New Orleans food", blasé beef eaters
bellow it's "just another meat market", and an "overpriced" one at that.

Siamese Restaurant　　　∇　25　14　18　$23
6601 Veterans Memorial Blvd. (Downs Blvd.), 504-454-8752;
www.siamesecuisine.com
"Absolutely delicious" curries, noodles and seafood
"burst with flavor" approaching "culinary serendipity" at
this Metairie Thai; enthusiasts easily overlook the "awful
strip-mall location" and "hilariously bad decor" since it's a
Bangkok-style "bargain."

Singha Ⓢ　　　　23　12　19　$15
(aka Singha Thai Cafe)
413 Carondelet St. (bet. Perdido & Poydras Sts.),
504-581-2205
At lunchtime, this CBD "hole-in-the-wall" is "hotter
than an oven" and "packed" with office workers han-
kering for a "quick" fix of skillfully "spiced", "tasty"
Thai dishes "with some zip"; the "friendly" staff "re-
members regulars", "fast service" means you "never

wait long" and the bill is "reasonable", making this canteen highly "popular."

Slice ⊠
23 | 17 | 17 | $14

(aka Slice Pizzeria)

1513 St. Charles Ave. (Melpomene Ave.), 504-525-7437

This Lower Garden District home of "good, chewy, gooey" pizza by the slice or by the pie, with "generous, high-quality toppings" and a "crisp crust", "looks like a tiny take-out place but widens in back" for casual, "inexpensive" meals; adding dash to the ambiance is a "hip crowd – and sometimes overly hip service."

Slim Goodies Diner ⊟
17 | 15 | 15 | $12

3322 Magazine St. (Toledano St.), 504-891-3447; www.slimgoodies.com

"Classic diner" meets "crunchy vegetarian" at this "offbeat" Garden District hangout where "stick-to-your-ribs" breakfasts and quirky plate lunches served by "tattooed waitresses" satisfy sleepy souls "in their jammies"; most agree it's a "hangover helper" that's hardly "slimming", but just right after a "late night out."

Smilie's Restaurant
15 | 13 | 16 | $23

5725 Jefferson Hwy. (Edwards Ave.), 504-733-3000; www.smiliesrestaurant.com

"You might run into Barnaby Jones or Jim Rockford" at this Harahan "'70s throwback" serving Creole and Italian fare among an eclectic menu that's sure to "fatten you up"; while a slew of scowlers scoff "they really know how to use a can opener" and the "ambiance makes retirement centers look hip", the low tabs and "natives who love the place" mean it keeps on ticking.

St. Charles Tavern ◑
14 | 8 | 14 | $14

1433 St. Charles Ave. (bet. Martin Luther King Jr. Blvd. & Thalia St.), 504-523-9823

"If you get a red-meat craving at 3 AM", you can convene with "a great cast of characters" at this 24-hour "dirty spoon dive", a "funky, friendly" Uptowner that tames booze-fueled hunger pangs with "bargain" "diner food" that's "better than you would expect" – just don't expect too much, and "don't let your shoestrings touch the floor."

STELLA!
28 | 25 | 26 | $56

Hôtel Provincial, 1032 Chartres St. (bet. St. Philip & Ursuline Sts.), 504-587-0091; www.restaurantstella.com

"Incredibly ambitious" chef Scott Boswell crafts an "innovative" New American menu starring "superlative" "experimental Creole fare" with "surprising flavor combinations", making this "intimate" hotel dining room and patio "tucked away in the Quarter" "worth the exclamation point"; if some cry "expensive", others are "shouting 'Stella!' all night" after their "memorable meal."

Steve's Diner ⊠   ▽ 20 11 17 $11
828 Gravier St. (bet. Baronne & Carondelet Sts.),
504-522-8198
"Downtown workers frequent" this "fast", "cafeteria-
style" eatery ("it's not a diner, it's a CBD lunchtime spot!")
serving meatloaf, catfish and other "homestyle" plates;
the specials offer a "different experience daily", while service remains consistently "prompt and polite."

Streetcar Bistro, The   – – – M
Baronne Plaza Hotel, 201 Baronne St. (Common St.),
504-565-5455; www.streetcarbistro.com
"Gustatory delights" surprise guests at this plainly furnished CBD hotel venue where chef Cris Pasia, a onetime
apprentice of Paul Prudhomme, largely pulls off a "hard-
to-believe" fusion with his "deft, contemporary" Asian-
Cajun cooking (think barbecued duck Napoleon and
sesame-crusted oysters); nearby execs "love it for lunch."

Sugar Park Tavern Ⓜ⊟   ▽ 23 8 16 $13
800 France St. (Dauphine St.), 504-940-6226; www.sugarpark.com
It's a "dive bar" in Bywater, but it's also "a destination" for
"damn good", "super-thin-crust" pizza with "sauce that
has a New Orleans kick"; the faithful flock here, unfazed
by the "seedy" surroundings ("decor, schmecor") and
"nonexistent service"; alternatively, you can get your
"bargain" pie delivered – "if they answer the phone", that is.

Sun Ray Grill ⊠   20 17 18 $24
1051 Annunciation St. (Andrew Higgins Dr.), 504-566-0021
Meadow Crest Ctr., 2600 Belle Chasse Hwy. (Mel Ott Park),
504-391-0053
3700 Orleans Ave. (Taft Pl.), 504-324-9663
619 Pink St. (Aris Ave.), 504-837-0055
www.sunraygrill.com
A "tasty", "eclectic" New American menu that borrows
licks from Tex-Mex and Asian cuisines, plus "specialty
cocktails" and a "casual" atmosphere, make this "cool"
quartet popular for group get-togethers; while "hefty portions" prove the "value" for some, the "hit-or-miss" quality
and service mean that many only "go if it's convenient."

Superior Grill   19 18 18 $21
3636 St. Charles Ave. (Antonine St.), 504-899-4200;
www.superiorgrill.com
"Bring a sombrero and a designated driver" to this Uptown
link in a Southern chain serving "strong", "abnormally
large margaritas" and "decent" Mexican standards like
fajitas, burritos and nachos that "would make Beavis
proud"; whether or not it's Mardi Gras – when the porch
overlooking St. Charles Avenue makes it prime for parade-
watching – the daily happy hour can expand into a "meat
market of epic proportions."

Surrey's Juice Bar ⓂⲎ   22 | 16 | 17 | $15
1418 Magazine St. (Euterpe St.), 504-524-3828
"Refreshing" juices squeezed to order, root beer on tap and a "healthy", "homemade" selection of American breakfast and lunch items are complemented by the "cute, hippie-type atmosphere" at this Lower Garden District "secret" for the "hangover set"; pop-ins say the only pip is a "cash-only" policy and "long waits" for weekend brunch.

Table One NEW   21 | 22 | 19 | $39
2800 Magazine St. (Washington Ave.), 504-872-9035
An "inviting" Garden District newcomer "in a great old building with exposed-brick walls and fireplaces", this upscale Creole-French bistro sports a bustling bar and dining room downstairs, topped by a more "elegant" upper level; but reviewers are not of one mind about the experience: while many admire veteran chef Gerard Maras' "well-executed", "original" dishes, critics carp "it seems like you're paying for a special meal, and it never really turns out that special", especially given the "haphazard service."

Taj Mahal Indian Cuisine   21 | 17 | 18 | $26
923 Metairie Rd. (Rosa Ave.), 504-836-6859
"Lots of aromatic spices" perfume the "real" Indian fare at this "nestled"-away Old Metairie mainstay run by the "wonderful" Keswani family, "who've put their heart and soul" into the place for 24 years; though several sigh "since the storm, the food's gone down", most diners still deem the $6.95 weekday lunch buffet a "good deal", especially given the variety of "vegetarian curries and biryanis."

Tan Dinh Ⲏ   ▽ 25 | 12 | 18 | $16
2005 Belle Chasse Hwy. (20th St.), 504-361-8008
"They close too early" wail worshipers of the "delicious" beef brisket pho, roasted quail and vermicelli salad bowls at this Gretna Vietnamese, "far and away, the best – and cheapest" in town; fans even forgive the florescent-lit cafeterialike quarters ("the former smaller location was far more charming").

Taqueria Corona   22 | 13 | 17 | $15
1827 Hickory Ave. (Citrus Rd.), 504-738-6722
5932 Magazine St. (bet. Eleonore & State Sts.),
504-897-3974
The Esplanade, 3535 Severn Ave. (W. Esplanade Ave.),
504-885-5088 🅢
"Adventurous" dishes "done right" ("try the tongue taco" or a *cebollita,* a cooked whole green onion) and "top-shelf" margaritas are the reasons besotted locals love to "pig out" at this "boisterous" family-run Mexican trio; the homespun fare is "authentic" and "cheap" enough to trump the "divey" digs.

Taqueros Ⓢ   18 19 17 $32
1432 St. Charles Ave. (Melpomene Ave.), 504-525-9996
The owners no doubt "spent a fortune renovating" the 19th-century Lower Garden District building housing this relocated Mexican, an upscale enclave decked with stucco walls, hardwood floors and Spanish tiles; its "ambitious" menu of both "classic" and "inventive" dishes delights disciples, but many miss the "dingy" Kenner locale and its low prices, since "high-style" guac and chips are "a hard sell in New Orleans."

Theo's   23 16 18 $15
4218 Magazine St. (Milan St.), 504-894-8554;
www.theospizza.com
"Wild toppings" and "crisp, buttery" thin crusts are what make this Uptown St. Louis–style pizzeria "unique"; the "college pie shop" decor and counter-only service are "nothing fancy" and pizzas made to order "can take a little time", but believers shrug "you can't rush perfection."

13 Monaghan ●   21 17 20 $12
517 Frenchmen St. (bet. Chartres & Decatur Sts.), 504-942-1345;
www.13monaghan.com
"Tater-tots with cheese and a cold beer hit the spot" at this Eclectic "late-night" Frenchmen Street bar and grill serving "simple repasts" with "lots of vegetarian options", "breakfast all day" and other "guilty pleasures"; an "insider's place", it attracts a crowd of music-loving "New Orleans characters" who lend it a "very relaxed" vibe.

Tommy's Cuisine ⓈSE   25 23 24 $44
746 Tchoupitoulas St. (bet. Girod & Julia Sts.), 504-581-1103;
www.tommyscuisine.com
"What a treat!" shout fans of this "knockout" Warehouse District Creole-Italian, where owner Tommy Andrade (ex Irene's) has "captured a loyal local following" with "outstanding" dishes served by an "educated" staff that "hardly ever misses a beat"; "dim lighting" and "warm", homey decor also help make this "a great place to be alone with someone special"; N.B. an offshoot wine bar that also serves imported cheeses recently opened next door.

Tony Mandina's ⓈⓂ   23 17 23 $23
1915 Pratt St. (Porter St.), 504-362-2010;
www.tonymandinas.com
"Galactic portions" of "consistently good", "reasonably priced" Southern Italian fare lure West Bankers to this "cozy" Gretna spot, where "the owners make you feel right at home"; "excellent service" prevails, and a live pianist entertains Friday and Saturday (the only nights that dinner is served), putting "the finishing touch" on a warm, "wonderful evening."

Trey Yuen 24 | 24 | 21 | $26
2100 N. Morrison Blvd. (W. University Ave.), Hammond,
985-345-6789
600 N. Causeway Blvd. (Monroe St.), Mandeville, 985-626-4476 Ⓜ
www.treyyuen.com
Most agree it's "worth crossing the lake" for these
Hammond and Mandeville Mandarins, where the Wong
brothers imbue Chinese fare with a "distinctly Louisiana
flair", using only the "freshest possible" ingredients; "attentive" service is a plus, and those struck by the "beautiful" surroundings – staged with "serene" koi ponds,
bamboo gardens, antiques and historical costumes –
promise it's "just like traveling to China."

Trolley Stop Cafe 16 | 9 | 17 | $12
1923 St. Charles Ave. (St. Andrew St.), 504-523-0090
"Good food with attitude" keeps crack-of-dawn wakers and
"every cop and cabbie in town" coming back to this "basic",
"non-touristy" Lower Garden District diner; a "cheap"
breakfast (also available for lunch) is the meal of choice,
and the "quick", "fun" waiters are real "characters."

Tujague's 21 | 19 | 21 | $37
823 Decatur St. (Madison St.), 504-525-8676; www.tujagues.com
This "dark and mysterious" 150-year-old French Quarter
Creole "institution" entices with a "steal" of a six-course
table d'hôte menu anchored by "worth-the-visit" beef
brisket topped with "zippy" horseradish sauce; if a
few find the whole package "kind of tired", more appreciate that it "never changes"; P.S. in-the-know locals
beat the set-price system by heading to "one of the last
remaining stand-up bars" in NOLA to enjoy generous
brisket po' boys.

Two Sisters Ⓩ⊘ – | – | – | I
223 N. Derbigny St. (N. Claiborne Ave.), 504-524-0056
The motto at this elemental Treme old-timer dishing Cajun,
Creole and soul sustenance is 'the town's best food and
lowest prices', and who could argue when you can chow
down on turkey necks (or wings) with rice, shrimp with
okra or a smothered pork chop for $7.50; while the photo of
the owner with Rosa Parks strikes a cord, the otherwise
downscale digs don't encourage lingering at this always-
packed, cash-only breakfast/lunch shack.

Two Tony's Ⓩ Ⓜ ▽ 23 | 15 | 20 | $24
(aka Il Tony's)
105 Hammond Hwy. (Lake Pontchartrain & 17th St. Canal),
504-831-0999; www.two-tonys.com
"Yep, they're still there" say relieved fans of this "friendly"
favorite at the edge of storm-ravaged Bucktown; it may
look like a "typical neighborhood" place, but the namesake father and son duo creates "quality" "New Orleans–

style Italian food" that's "reasonably priced" to boot, ensuring that most diners leave "completely satisfied."

Ugly Dog Saloon & BBQ   19 | 10 | 15 | $15
401 Andrew Higgins Dr. (Tchoupitoulas St.), 504-569-8459; www.uglydogsaloon.net
Swine seekers "won't be disappointed" at this Warehouse District barbecue pit revered for "awesome" portions of smokin' spareribs plus burgers, brisket and comforting sides like chili beans "swimming in sour cream and cheese"; the "sports-bar atmosphere" is "anything but fancy", but neither are the tabs, and it's a perfect place to "relax and watch the game."

UPPERLINE Ⓜ   26 | 24 | 25 | $45
1413 Upperline St. (bet. Prytania St. & St. Charles Ave.), 504-891-9822; www.upperline.com
"Wonderful chef" Ken Smith and "consummate hostess" JoAnn Clevenger have "kept the torch lit" at this "quirky" Uptowner, serving "splendid", "inventive" Contemporary Louisiana cuisine with the option of an "excellent" seven-course 'Taste of New Orleans' menu; on par with the food is the setting inside a lofty 1877 house, whose four dining rooms are decorated with paintings from Clevenger's collection and graced by "fine", "cordial service."

Vega Tapas Cafe Ⓢ   22 | 21 | 21 | $34
2051 Metairie Rd. (bet. Beverly Garden Dr. & Bonnabel Blvd.), 504-836-2007; www.vegatapascafe.com
"Every little dish is special" according to admirers of this Old Metairie Med, which keeps things fresh with seasonal small plates and ever-changing exhibits of "funky" art for sale; "helpful" waiters and a "cool atmosphere" with "beautiful Moroccan" touches add to its appeal but don't stop some from grumbling about petite portions at "big prices."

Venezia Ⓢ   20 | 13 | 17 | $20
587 Central Ave. (1 block north of Jefferson Hwy.), 504-734-3991
A "great place to pig out" say boosters of this Jefferson spin-off of the now-closed Mid-City original, which adds some New Orleans zing to "gourmet" pizzas and "tasty traditional" Italian dishes; "huge portions", "reasonable prices" and service with "a smile" are more reasons why its cabinlike digs are "always packed."

Veranda   ▽ 21 | 21 | 21 | $38
Hotel InterContinental, 444 St. Charles Ave. (Poydras St.), 504-585-4383; www.new-orleans.intercontinental.com
Fans forgive the misleading moniker (a glass-enclosed courtyard, not a veranda, is the airy attraction) at this CBD Continental, and simply relish that its "famous" Sunday jazz brunch with unlimited champagne is "finally back", along with the "terrific" lunch buffet; a few are less bubbly, however, finding this "fancy" hotel eatery "could be in any city."

Vincent's
23 | 18 | 21 | $33

4411 Chastant St. (Transcontinental Dr.), 504-885-2984 ☒
7839 St. Charles Ave. (Fern St.), 504-866-9313 Ⓜ
www.vincentsitaliancuisine.com

"Rich" specialties like "superb veal cannelloni" and corn-crab bisque worth "walking through broken glass to eat" cast a Southern Italian spell at this red and gold, "back-in-time" Metairie mainstay and its smaller but equally "popular" Uptown *fratello* where "dressed-to-the-nines couples sit next to college kids"; despite "long waits", the reward is a "romantic" atmosphere that also "feels like home", especially if you are − or are into − "old-style" Sicilian.

VIZARD'S
ON THE AVENUE ☒ Ⓜ NEW
27 | 24 | 25 | $48

Garden District Hotel, 2203 St. Charles Ave. (Jackson Ave.), 504-529-9912

Foodies, socialites, "movers and shakers" swarm to this "lively" post-Katrina newcomer inside the Garden District Hotel, eager to tuck into veteran chef Kevin Vizard's "spellbinding", "superb" Creole-Mediterranean fare; its "chic" ambiance and "pleasant" staff also help make it "worth" the expense − particularly if you nab "a table looking out on the avenue"; N.B. reservations strongly suggested.

Voodoo BBQ
17 | 12 | 14 | $16

1501 St. Charles Ave. (Martin Luther King Jr. Blvd.), 504-522-4647
100 James Dr. E. (Airline Rd.), St. Rose, 504-464-1880
www.voodoobbqandgrill.com

"Starving students on a budget" and other smoke-seekers appreciate the "tangy barbecue in three different styles" − Caribbean, Carolina and Texas − at this "corporate funky" duo that's survived in a city where "BBQ joints never make it"; the St. Rose location has a child-friendly setting and a fuller menu, but familiars warn "don't go for the ambiance" − or expect more than "average" 'cue − at the counter-service Lower Garden District branch.

Wasabi ☒
23 | 16 | 19 | $25

900 Frenchmen St. (Burgundy St.), 504-943-9433;
www.wasabirestaurant.com

"Exceptional" entrees and "delectable" sushi with a "creative" touch make this "unpretentious" Japanese "hole-in-the-wall" a "great li'l Marigny oasis" despite "video poker machines at the door" and slightly "airheaded" service; if that sounds off-putting, "they deliver" too.

Whole Foods Market
23 | 19 | 21 | $16

5600 Magazine St. (Arabella St.), 504-899-9119
3420 Veterans Memorial Hwy. (Severn Ave.), 504-888-8225
www.wholefoods.com

It's "technically" a "pricey", "top-of-the-line" grocery store, but "fresh", "delicious" prepared foods, salads and other "ready-made meal options" cause "limousine liberals" to crowd these Uptown and Metairie branches of the national chain for dinner and lunch; Magazine Street has a patio and indoor counter seating, while the larger Metairie store boasts a cafe, cheese tastings and a gelateria; a few disgruntled diners insist "the fare looks better than it tastes."

Willie Mae's Scotch House 🗷 🅼   _ | _ | _ | I
2401 St. Ann St. (N. Tonti St.)
If all goes according to plan, determined 90-year-old chef-owner Willie Mae Seaton will be back behind her stove by January 2007 at this Mid-City soul food shrine, a cherished hole-in-the-wall destroyed by the flood, rebuilt by volunteers and fans, and marked with the same '50s-era sign; it will once again point the way to such wonders as fried chicken spiked with red pepper, white beans and bread pudding, served family-style in a no-frills dining room at a famously lackadaisical pace.

Wolfe's in the Warehouse 🆕   _ | _ | _ | E
New Orleans Marriott at the Convention Ctr., 859 Convention Center Blvd. (St. Joseph St.), 504-613-2882
Peristyle's Tom Wolfe is the maestro behind the menu in this sharp new hotel dining room across from the Convention Center; its high-end Creole cuisine embraces duck and syrup-glazed pork chops for dinner and lighter sandwiches and salads for lunch, all complemented by the traditional decor of a black-and-white tile floor, ceiling fans and wrought-iron fixtures.

Ye Olde College Inn 🗷 🅼   18 | 16 | 19 | $19
3000 S. Carrollton Ave. (bet. Earhart Blvd. & Fig St.), 504-866-3683
"A New Orleans tradition" since 1933, this Southern-Creole in Carrollton moved into roomier, more "upscale" digs next door after Katrina, and the "good as ever" menu's been schooled too – with "upgrades" like bacon and Havarti on the fried oyster po' boy; though some feel the "pricier" place hasn't recaptured its old "neighborhood joint glory", many still prize its "very local", "colorful" and "congenial" atmosphere, preserved under owner John Blancher of Rock 'n' Bowl, as well as its distinctive details – including the mural depicting Canal Street in the '60s.

Young's 🗷 🅼   ▽ 25 | 15 | 22 | $44
850 Robert Blvd. (Marche Blvd.), Slidell, 985-643-9331
"If you don't know it, you won't find" this family-run Slidell steakhouse (there's "no sign outside") where meat lovers munch on "excellent" beef so "high-quality" "you can cut it with a fork"; even those who think "the prices are high" say "the service" (if not the surroundings) "more than makes up for it."

Zea Café　　　　　　　22　20　20　$23
1655 Hickory Ave. (Citrus Rd.), 504-738-0799
Zea Rotisserie
1525 St. Charles Ave. (Terpsichore St.), 504-520-8100
Zea Rotisserie & Brewery
Clearview Shopping Ctr., 4450 Veterans Memorial Blvd.
(Clearview Pkwy.), 504-780-9090
Zea Rotisserie & Grill
Esplanade Mall, 1401 W. Esplanade Ave. (Arizona Ave.),
504-468-7733
www.zearestaurants.com
Locals "love, love, love the corn grits" (a "standout") at
this upbeat Eclectic mini-chain where the "tasty" dishes
include equally "addictive" Thai ribs, "excellent" salads
and a variety of rotisserie meats, all in "huge portions";
beer drinkers give a thumbs-up to the branch in Metairie's
Clearview mall, which doubles as a "great" microbrewery.

Zeke's ⏹　　　　　　17　13　20　$21
1517 Metairie Rd. (Bonnabel Blvd.), 504-832-1133
Although locals lament "it's not the same" since beloved
singing owner Zeke Unangst died, this "unpretentious"
"seafood joint" in an Old Metairie strip mall (now run by
Franky & Johnny's Darryl Cortello) hasn't changed its
menu of "good cheap eats"; it's "not a destination restaurant", but still draws everyone from "empty-nesters" to
"preppy young families" to neighborhood "codgers";
N.B. closes at 9 PM most nights, 10 PM Fridays.

Zoë　　　　　　　　20　22　21　$41
W New Orleans, 2nd fl., 333 Poydras St. (S. Peters St.),
504-207-5018
"Wear black" to this "smashing"-looking W hotel eatery in
the CBD, a "hip" business-lunch oasis with "gracious"
service; the Contemporary Louisiana cuisine prompts ar-
gument among arbiters of taste – some judge it "creative",
while others rule against "wacky combinations" that are,
"not surprisingly, overpriced."

Restaurant Indexes

CUISINES
LOCATIONS
SPECIAL FEATURES

CUISINES

American (New)
Bayona
Dakota, The
Etoile
Fire
Herbsaint
Iris
Le Parvenu
New Orleans Grill
One Restaurant
Pelican Club
Savvy Gourmet
Stella!
Sun Ray Grill

American (Traditional)
Betsy's Pancake
Bubba Gump
Cannon's
Coffee Pot
Come Back Inn
Ernst Cafe
Feelings Cafe
GB's Patio B&G
Gordon Biersch
Hard Rock Cafe
Home Furnishings
Houston's
Mother's
O'Henry's
Oscar's
P&G
Parasol's
Popeyes
Port of Call
Raising Cane's
Slim Goodies
St. Charles Tavern
Surrey's Juice Bar

Argentinean
La Boca

Asian
Azul
Mike's on the Ave.

Sara's
Streetcar Bistro

Bakeries
Croissant d'Or
La Boulangerie
La Madeleine

Barbecue
Bywater BBQ
Corky's BBQ
Hillbilly BBQ
Joint, The
Ugly Dog Saloon
Voodoo BBQ

Belgian
Clementine's

Cajun
Alpine, The
Bon Ton Café
Cafe Beignet
Cafe Giovanni
Cafe Pontalba
Cochon
Coop's Place
Copeland's
Domilise's
Franky & Johnny's
K-Paul's
La Thai
Mother's
Mulate's
New Orleans Food
Oak Alley
Petunia's
Rest. des Familles
Schiro's
Streetcar Bistro
Two Sisters

Californian
Fire
Lucy's

Chinese
(* dim sum specialist)
August Moon
Café East
China Doll
Five Happiness
Great Wall
Kim Son
P.F. Chang's
Royal China*
Trey Yuen

Coffeehouses
Café Du Monde
Caffe! Caffe!
CC's Coffee
Chateau Coffee
Churros Café
Coffea Gallery
Morning Call
PJ's Coffee
Royal Blend
rue de la course

Coffee Shops/Diners
Bluebird Cafe
Clover Grill
Coffee Cottage
Coffee Rani
Elizabeth's
Frosty's Café
Russell's Marina
Slim Goodies
Steve's Diner
Trolley Stop Cafe

Contemporary Louisiana
Anatole
Bank Cafe
Brigtsen's
Calas Bistro
Crescent City Brew
Dakota, The
Dante's Kitchen
Emeril's
Gulfstream St. Charles
Jackson

La Louisiane
La Petite Grocery
Mat & Naddie's
NOLA
Peristyle
Ralph's on Park
7 on Fulton
Upperline
Zoë

Continental
August
Cuvée
Flaming Torch
Rib Room
Veranda

Creole
Abita Brew Pub
Alpine, The
Anatole
Antoine's
Arnaud's
Begue's
Brennan's
Broussard's
Café Adelaide
Cafe Atchafalaya
Cafe Pontalba
Clancy's
Coffee Pot
Commander's Palace
Copeland's
Court of Two Sisters
Crystal Room
Cuvée
Dante's Kitchen
Dick & Jenny's
Domilise's
Dunbar's Creole
Eleven 79
Emeril's Delmonico
Feelings Cafe
Fury's
Galatoire's
Gumbo Shop
Home Furnishings

Ignatius Eatery
Jacques-Imo's
Joey K's
Juan's Flying Burrito
La Côte Brasserie
Le Parvenu
Li'l Dizzy's Cafe
Liuzza's by Track
Mimi's
Mr. Ed's
Muriel's Jackson Sq.
Napoleon House
NOLA
Oak Alley
Olivier's
Palace Café
Petunia's
Ralph's on Park
Remoulade
Riccobono's Peppermill
Sal & Judy's
Sara's
Schiro's
Smilie's
Table One
Tommy's Cuisine
Tujague's
Two Sisters
Two Tony's
Upperline
Vizard's on the Ave.
Wolfe's in Warehouse
Ye Olde College Inn

Cuban
Azul
Churros Café
Country Flame
Liborio Cuban

Dessert
Angelo Brocato
Café Du Monde
Caffe! Caffe!
Coffee Cottage
Coffee Rani
Croissant d'Or
Dong Phuong

Hansen's Sno-Bliz
La Crêpe Nanou
La Madeleine
Morning Call
rue de la course

Eclectic
Abita Brew Pub
Cafe Rani
Dick & Jenny's
Jazmine Café
Marigny Brasserie
Semolina Pasta
Semolina's Bistro
13 Monaghan
Whole Foods
Zea

Fondue
Melting Pot

French
Broussard's
Flaming Torch
Galatoire's
La Côte Brasserie
La Provence
Peristyle
Riche

French (Bistro)
Alberta
Café Degas
Chateau du Lac
Delachaise, The
Etoile
La Crêpe Nanou
La Madeleine
La Petite Grocery
Lilette
Martinique Bistro
Meauxbar
Table One

French (New)
August
Begue's
Crystal Room

Dominique's
Herbsaint
Longbranch, The

Greek
Acropolis
Mr. Gyros

Hamburgers
Beachcorner B&G
Bud's Broiler
Clover Grill
GB's Patio B&G
Gordon Biersch
Hard Rock Cafe
Lee's Hamburgers
New Orleans Hamburger
O'Henry's
Oscar's
Port of Call

Health Food
Apple Seed
Whole Foods

Honduran
Jazz Tacos

Ice Cream Parlors
Angelo Brocato
Hansen's Sno-Bliz

Indian
Nirvana Indian
Taj Mahal

Italian
(N=Northern; S=Southern)
Adolfo's (S)
Andrea's (N)
Anselmo's (S)
Bacco
Bravo! Cucina
Brick Oven Cafe
Cafe DiBlasi
Cafe Giovanni
Cafe Roma
Carmine's
Civello's

Eleven 79
Fausto's Bistro
Fazzio's
Fiorella's Café (S)
Fury's
Impastato's
Irene's Cuisine (S)
Italian Pie
Liuzza's Restaurant
Louisiana Pizza
Maple St. Cafe
Mimi's
Mona Lisa
Mosca's
Mr. Ed's
Nardo's Trattoria (N)
Nuvolari's
Pascal's Manale
R & O's
Riccobono's Peppermill
Ristorante Da Piero (N)
Ristorante Filippo
Sal & Judy's (S)
Semolina Pasta
Semolina's Bistro
Smilie's
Tommy's Cuisine
Tony Mandina's (S)
Two Tony's
Venezia
Vincent's (S)

Japanese
(* sushi specialist)
Brothers Sushi*
Hana Japanese*
Horinoya
Jipang*
Kyoto
Kyoto II
Little Tokyo*
Miyako*
NINJA*
Rock-n-Sake*
Sake Cafe
Shogun
Wasabi*

Kosher
Casablanca
Kosher Cajun Deli

Lebanese
Lebanon's Café

Mediterranean
Acropolis
Angeli on Decatur
Bank Cafe
Fellini's
Fresco Cafe
Jamila's Cafe
Maple St. Cafe
Napoleon House
Vega Tapas
Vizard's on the Ave.

Mexican
Carreta's Grill
Casa Garcia
Country Flame
Fiesta Bistro
Juan's Flying Burrito
Lucy's
Nacho Mama's
Superior Grill
Taqueria Corona
Taqueros

Middle Eastern
Babylon Café
Byblos
Mona's Cafe

Moroccan
Casablanca

Nuevo Latino
Serrano's Salsa

Pan-Latin
Pupuseria Macarena

Pizza
Angeli on Decatur
Cafe Roma
Fresco Cafe
Italian Pie

Louisiana Pizza
Mark Twain's Pizza
New York Pizza
R & O's
Reginelli's
Slice
Sugar Park Tavern
Theo's
Venezia

Po' Boys
Cafe Maspero
Central Grocery
Come Back Inn
Crabby Jack's
Deanie's Seafood
Domilise's
Franky & Johnny's
Galley
Ignatius Eatery
Joey K's
Mike Serio's
Parasol's
Parkway Bakery
Russell's Short Stop

Pub Food
Beachcorner B&G
Gordon Biersch
Sugar Park Tavern

Sandwiches
Audubon Park
Cafe Maspero
Central Grocery
Crabby Jack's
DiMartino's
Domilise's
Kosher Cajun Deli
Martin Wine Cellar
Mike Serio's
Roly Poly
Russell's Short Stop
Whole Foods

Seafood
Acme Oyster
Andrea's
Arnaud's
Besh Steak

Bourbon House
Bozo's
Bubba Gump
Cafe Beignet
Cannon's
Carmine's
Casamento's
Crabby Jack's
Deanie's Seafood
Don's Seafood
Drago's
Franky & Johnny's
Galley
GW Fins
Harbor Seafood
Jack Dempsey's
Joey K's
Landry's Seafood
Martinique Bistro
Middendorf's
Mimi's
Minnie's Catfish
New Orleans Food
New Orleans Hamburger
Pascal's Manale
R & O's
Red Fish Grill
Rest. des Familles
RioMar
Saltwater Grill
Tony Mandina's
Trey Yuen
Two Tony's
Zeke's

Small Plates
(See also Spanish tapas specialist)
Cochon (Cajun)
Delachaise, The (French)
Herbsaint (New American)
Mike's on the Ave. (Asian)
Vega Tapas (Med.)

Soul Food
Fiorella's Café
Jacques-Imo's
Minnie's Catfish

Praline Connection
Two Sisters
Willie Mae's

Southern
Cafe Atchafalaya
Café Reconcile
Coop's Place
Eat
Elizabeth's
Praline Connection
Ye Olde College Inn

Spanish
(* tapas specialist)
Fiesta Bistro*
Laurentino's Tapas*
Liborio Cuban
Lola's
Madrid*
RioMar*

Steakhouses
Besh Steak
Crazy Johnnie's
Dickie Brennan's
La Boca
Morton's
Mr. John's
Rib Room
Ruth's Chris
Shula's
Young's

Tex-Mex
Cuco's

Thai
Bangkok Thai
Basil Leaf
La Thai
Siamese
Singha

Tunisian
Jamila's Cafe

Vegetarian
Apple Seed
Bennachin

Cafe Atchafalaya
Cafe Rani
Coffee Rani
Fellini's
Jazmine Café
Nirvana Indian
Slim Goodies
Taj Mahal
13 Monaghan
Whole Foods

Vietnamese
August Moon
Dong Phuong

Frosty's Café
Jazmine Café
Kim Son
Nine Roses
Pho Bang
Pho Tau Bay
Tan Dinh

West African
Bennachin

LOCATIONS

NEW ORLEANS

Bucktown
R & O's
Two Tony's

Bywater
Bywater BBQ
Coffea Gallery
Elizabeth's
Jack Dempsey's
Joint, The
Schiro's
Sugar Park Tavern

Carrollton
Basil Leaf
Fiesta Bistro
Five Happiness
Iris
Jacques-Imo's
Jazmine Café
Lebanon's Café
Maple St. Cafe
Mat & Naddie's
NINJA
One Restaurant
rue de la course
Saltwater Grill
Ye Olde College Inn

CBD (Central Business District)
Anatole
Apple Seed
August
Besh Steak
Bon Ton Café
Café Adelaide
Crystal Room
Cuvée
Gordon Biersch
Horinoya
Italian Pie
Jipang
Liborio Cuban

Mike Serio's
Mother's
New Orleans Grill
O'Henry's
P&G
Riche
Roly Poly
Shula's
Singha
Steve's Diner
Streetcar Bistro
Veranda
Zoë

Central City
Café Reconcile
Minnie's Catfish

Chalmette
Cafe Roma

Destrehan
Bud's Broiler

Faubourg Marigny
Adolfo's
Bank Cafe
Feelings Cafe
Marigny Brasserie
Mona's Cafe
Praline Connection
Semolina Pasta
13 Monaghan
Wasabi

Faubourg St. John
Café Degas
Ralph's on Park

French Quarter
Acme Oyster
Alpine, The
Angeli on Decatur
Antoine's
Arnaud's

Bacco
Bayona
Begue's
Bennachin
Bourbon House
Brennan's
Broussard's
Bubba Gump
Cafe Beignet
Café Du Monde
Cafe Giovanni
Cafe Maspero
Cafe Pontalba
Cafe Roma
Central Grocery
Clover Grill
Coffee Pot
Coop's Place
Country Flame
Court of Two Sisters
Crescent City Brew
Croissant d'Or
Dickie Brennan's
Dominique's
Eat
Fiorella's Café
Galatoire's
Gumbo Shop
GW Fins
Hard Rock Cafe
Irene's Cuisine
Jazz Tacos
K-Paul's
La Louisiane
Landry's Seafood
Louisiana Pizza
Meauxbar
Mona Lisa
Morton's
Muriel's Jackson Sq.
Napoleon House
NOLA
Olivier's
Palace Café
Pelican Club
Peristyle
Petunia's

PJ's Coffee
Port of Call
Red Fish Grill
Reginelli's
Remoulade
Rib Room
Royal Blend
Stella!
Tujague's

Garden District
Brothers Sushi
Cafe Atchafalaya
Cannon's
CC's Coffee
Commander's Palace
Joey K's
Mike's on the Ave.
Parasol's
Reginelli's
rue de la course
Sake Cafe
Semolina's Bistro
Slim Goodies
Table One
Vizard's on the Ave.

Garden District (Lower)
Cafe Roma
Emeril's Delmonico
Gulfstream St. Charles
Home Furnishings
Jackson
Juan's Flying Burrito
Melting Pot
Miyako
Mr. John's
Popeyes
Slice
Surrey's Juice Bar
Taqueros
Trolley Stop Cafe
Voodoo BBQ
Zea

Gretna
Clementine's
DiMartino's

Kim Son
Nine Roses
O'Henry's
Pho Tau Bay
Sun Ray Grill
Tan Dinh
Tony Mandina's

Harahan/River Ridge
Coffee Cottage
Hillbilly BBQ
Kyoto II
La Madeleine
Mimi's
Reginelli's
Smilie's
Taqueria Corona
Zea

Jefferson
Crabby Jack's
Italian Pie
Venezia

Kenner
Brick Oven Cafe
Bud's Broiler
Calas Bistro
Chateau Coffee
Chateau du Lac
Fiesta Latina
Harbor Seafood
Italian Pie
Le Parvenu
Madrid
O'Henry's
Pupuseria Macarena
Ristorante Da Piero
Sake Cafe
Zea

Lakefront/Lakeview
Russell's Marina

Metairie
Acme Oyster
Acropolis
Andrea's
Anselmo's

Bozo's
Bravo! Cucina
Bud's Broiler
Byblos
Café East
Caffe! Caffe!
Carmine's
Carreta's Grill
Casablanca
Casa Garcia
Chateau Coffee
Churros Café
Come Back Inn
Corky's BBQ
Crazy Johnnie's
Cuco's
Deanie's Seafood
Don's Seafood
Drago's
Fausto's Bistro
Frosty's Café
Fury's
Houston's
Impastato's
Kosher Cajun Deli
Laurentino's Tapas
Lee's Hamburgers
Little Tokyo
Martin Wine Cellar
Miyako
Morning Call
Mr. Ed's
Mr. Gyros
Nacho Mama's
New Orleans Hamburger
P.F. Chang's
PJ's Coffee
Raising Cane's
Riccobono's Peppermill
Ristorante Filippo
Royal Blend
Royal China
Russell's Short Stop
Ruth's Chris
Sake Cafe
Semolina Pasta
Serrano's Salsa

Shogun
Siamese
Sun Ray Grill
Taqueria Corona
Vincent's
Whole Foods
Zea

Mid-City
Angelo Brocato
Beachcorner B&G
Betsy's Pancake
Fellini's
Italian Pie
Juan's Flying Burrito
Li'l Dizzy's Cafe
Liuzza's by Track
Liuzza's Restaurant
Lola's
Mona's Cafe
Parkway Bakery
Popeyes
Sun Ray Grill
Willie Mae's

New Orleans East
Dong Phuong
Pho Bang

Old Metairie
Byblos
Galley
Great Wall
La Thai
Mark Twain's Pizza
Oscar's
Taj Mahal
Vega Tapas
Zeke's

Riverbend
Bangkok Thai
Brigtsen's
Dante's Kitchen
GB's Patio B&G
Hana Japanese
La Madeleine
Louisiana Pizza

O'Henry's
Sara's

Treme
Two Sisters

Uptown
Alberta
Audubon Park
August Moon
Babylon Café
Bluebird Cafe
Byblos
Cafe Rani
Casamento's
Civello's
Clancy's
Delachaise, The
Dick & Jenny's
Domilise's
Dunbar's Creole
Flaming Torch
Franky & Johnny's
Fresco Cafe
Hansen's Sno-Bliz
Ignatius Eatery
Jamila's Cafe
Joint, The
Kyoto
La Boulangerie
La Crêpe Nanou
La Petite Grocery
Lilette
Martinique Bistro
Mona's Cafe
Nacho Mama's
Nardo's Trattoria
New York Pizza
Nirvana Indian
Pascal's Manale
PJ's Coffee
Popeyes
Reginelli's
Roly Poly
Savvy Gourmet
St. Charles Tavern
Superior Grill

Taqueria Corona
Theo's
Upperline
Vincent's
Whole Foods

Warehouse District
Azul
Cochon
Eleven 79
Emeril's
Ernst Cafe
Fire
Herbsaint
La Boca
La Côte Brasserie
Le Citron Bistro
Lucy's
Mulate's

RioMar
Rock-n-Sake
7 on Fulton
Sun Ray Grill
Tommy's Cuisine
Ugly Dog Saloon
Wolfe's in Warehouse

West Bank
Bud's Broiler
Cafe DiBlasi
China Doll
Copeland's
DiMartino's
New Orleans Food
Pho Bang
Popeyes
Rest. des Familles
Semolina Pasta

BEYOND NEW ORLEANS

Abita Springs/Covington
Abita Brew Pub
Coffee Rani
Copeland's
Dakota, The
Etoile
Longbranch, The
New Orleans Food
Semolina Pasta

Avondale
Mosca's

Houma
Copeland's

Lacombe
La Provence
Sal & Judy's

Manchac
Middendorf's

Mandeville/Hammond
Caffe! Caffe!
Carreta's Grill
Coffee Rani
Cuco's
Fazzio's
Little Tokyo
Nuvolari's
PJ's Coffee
Semolina Pasta
Trey Yuen

Slidell
Cuco's
Italian Pie
Young's

St. Rose
Voodoo BBQ

Vacherie
Oak Alley

SPECIAL FEATURES

(Indexes list the best in each category. Multi-location restaurants' features may vary by branch.)

Breakfast
(See also Hotel Dining)
Alpine, The
Audubon Park
Betsy's Pancake
Bluebird Cafe
Brennan's
Café Du Monde
Caffe! Caffe!
CC's Coffee
Chateau Coffee
Clover Grill
Coffee Cottage
Coffee Pot
Coffee Rani
Croissant d'Or
Elizabeth's
Jazmine Café
Joey K's
La Madeleine
Mike Serio's
Morning Call
Mother's
Nine Roses
Petunia's
Pho Tau Bay
PJ's Coffee
Riccobono's Peppermill
Royal Blend
rue de la course
Russell's Marina
Slim Goodies
St. Charles Tavern
Surrey's Juice Bar
Trolley Stop Cafe
Whole Foods

Brunch
Andrea's
Antoine's
Arnaud's
Audubon Park
Bank Cafe
Begue's
Brennan's
Bywater BBQ
Cafe Atchafalaya
Café Degas
Cafe Rani
Coffee Rani
Commander's Palace
Copeland's
Court of Two Sisters
Dante's Kitchen
Elizabeth's
Feelings Cafe
Flaming Torch
Jackson
La Côte Brasserie
La Provence
Marigny Brasserie
Martin Wine Cellar
Morning Call
Muriel's Jackson Sq.
Palace Café
Ralph's on Park
Rest. des Familles
Rib Room
Savvy Gourmet
Slim Goodies
Smilie's
Table One

Buffet Served
(Check availability)
Audubon Park
Begue's
Court of Two Sisters
La Côte Brasserie
Mat & Naddie's
Nirvana Indian
Rib Room
Royal China

Smilie's
Taj Mahal
Veranda

Business Dining
Andrea's
Antoine's
Arnaud's
August
Bacco
Bon Ton Café
Brennan's
Café Adelaide
Commander's Palace
Crystal Room
Cuvée
Dickie Brennan's
Emeril's
Emeril's Delmonico
Galatoire's
Gordon Biersch
GW Fins
Herbsaint
La Louisiane
La Petite Grocery
Morton's
Muriel's Jackson Sq.
New Orleans Grill
NOLA
Palace Café
Pelican Club
Peristyle
Ralph's on Park
Red Fish Grill
Rib Room
Ruth's Chris
Veranda
Zoë

BYO
Anatole
Babylon Café
Bennachin
Eat
Hillbilly BBQ
Jazmine Café
Joint, The

K-Paul's
La Petite Grocery
Lebanon's Café
Lola's
Marigny Brasserie
Mona's Cafe
Palace Café
Parkway Bakery
Pascal's Manale
Pelican Club
Peristyle
Pho Tau Bay
Praline Connection
Pupuseria Macarena
Ralph's on Park
Red Fish Grill
Reginelli's
Remoulade
Rest. des Familles
Rib Room
RioMar
Ristorante Da Piero
Ristorante Filippo
Rock-n-Sake
Ruth's Chris
Sake Cafe
Sal & Judy's
Sara's
Savvy Gourmet
Schiro's
Upperline

Celebrity Chefs
August, *John Besh*
Bayona, *Susan Spicer*
Besh Steak, *John Besh*
Brigtsen's, *Frank Brigtsen*
Café Adelaide, *Danny Trace*
Cochon, *Donald Link*
Commander's Palace, *Tory McPhail*
Cuvée, *Robert Iacovone*
Dominique's, *D. Macquet*
Emeril's, *Emeril Lagasse*
Emeril's Delmonico, *Emeril Lagasse*
Herbsaint, *Donald Link*

K-Paul's, *Paul Prudhomme*
La Provence, *Chris Kerageorgiou*
Lilette, *John Harris*
NOLA, *Emeril Lagasse*
Riche, *Todd English*
Stella!, *Scott Boswell*
Table One, *Gerard Maras*
Upperline, *Ken Smith*
Vizard's on the Ave., *Kevin Vizard*

Child-Friendly

(Alternatives to the usual fast-food places; * children's menu available)
Abita Brew Pub*
Acme Oyster*
Acropolis*
Andrea's*
Angeli on Decatur
Anselmo's*
Arnaud's
August Moon
Bacco
Bangkok Thai
Basil Leaf
Begue's
Bennachin
Betsy's Pancake*
Bluebird Cafe
Bon Ton Café
Bourbon House
Bozo's*
Bravo! Cucina*
Brennan's*
Brick Oven Cafe
Broussard's
Bubba Gump*
Byblos
Cafe Atchafalaya
Café Degas
Cafe DiBlasi*
Café Du Monde
Cafe Giovanni
Cafe Maspero
Cafe Pontalba*
Cafe Rani*
Café Reconcile
Caffe! Caffe!*
Cannon's*
Carreta's Grill*
Casablanca
Casa Garcia*
Chateau Coffee*
China Doll
Churros Café
Coffee Pot*
Coffee Rani*
Come Back Inn*
Commander's Palace
Copeland's*
Corky's BBQ*
Country Flame
Court of Two Sisters*
Crazy Johnnie's
Crescent City Brew*
Crystal Room*
Cuco's*
Dakota, The*
Dante's Kitchen
Deanie's Seafood*
DiMartino's*
Domilise's
Don's Seafood*
Drago's*
Elizabeth's
Fausto's Bistro
Fazzio's*
Fellini's
Fiorella's Café
Five Happiness
Franky & Johnny's*
Frosty's Café*
Fury's*
Galley*
GB's Patio B&G*
Gordon Biersch*
Harbor Seafood*
Hard Rock Cafe*
Houston's
Impastato's
Irene's Cuisine
Jacques-Imo's

Jamila's Cafe*
Joey K's*
Kim Son
Kyoto II*
La Madeleine*
Landry's Seafood*
Lee's Hamburgers*
Le Parvenu*
Liuzza's by Track
Louisiana Pizza*
Lucy's*
Marigny Brasserie
Martinique Bistro*
Mat & Naddie's
Middendorf's*
Mike Serio's
Mimi's*
Miyako*
Mona's Cafe*
Mosca's
Mother's*
Mr. Ed's*
Mr. Gyros*
Mr. John's
Mulate's*
Muriel's Jackson Sq.*
Nacho Mama's*
Napoleon House
New Orleans Food*
New Orleans Hamburger*
NINJA
Nuvolari's*
Oak Alley*
O'Henry's*
Olivier's
Palace Café*
Pascal's Manale*
Pelican Club*
R & O's*
Red Fish Grill*
Reginelli's
Remoulade
Rest. des Familles*
Rib Room*
Riccobono's Peppermill*
RioMar
Royal China

rue de la course
Russell's Marina*
Russell's Short Stop
Sake Cafe*
Sal & Judy's*
Saltwater Grill*
Semolina Pasta*
Semolina's Bistro*
Serrano's Salsa*
Shogun*
Siamese
Smilie's*
St. Charles Tavern*
Steve's Diner
Streetcar Bistro*
Sun Ray Grill*
Superior Grill*
Tan Dinh
Taqueria Corona
Tony Mandina's*
Trey Yuen*
Tujague's
Two Tony's*
Ugly Dog Saloon
Venezia*
Veranda*
Vincent's*
Voodoo BBQ*
Wasabi
Whole Foods
Ye Olde College Inn*
Young's*
Zea*
Zeke's*

Convention Center Convenience
Besh Steak
Café Adelaide
Eleven 79
Emeril's
Gordon Biersch
La Boca
La Côte Brasserie
Morton's
Mulate's
New Orleans Grill

RioMar
Rock-n-Sake
7 on Fulton
Tommy's Cuisine
Wolfe's in Warehouse

Dining Alone
(Other than hotels and places with counter service)
Byblos
Cafe Atchafalaya
Cafe Maspero
Cafe Pontalba
Cafe Rani
Caffe! Caffe!
Cochon
Domilise's
Jazmine Café
Joey K's
Lebanon's Café
Maple St. Cafe
Marigny Brasserie
Napoleon House
Nine Roses
NOLA
Pascal's Manale
Pelican Club
Port of Call
Saltwater Grill
Semolina Pasta
Taj Mahal
Taqueria Corona
Taqueros
Tujague's
Upperline

Entertainment
(Call for days and times of performances)
Alpine, The (jazz)
Andrea's (piano)
Begue's (piano)
Broussard's (piano)
Café East (Latin)
Cafe Giovanni (opera/piano)
Carreta's Grill (bands)
Civello's (opera)
Commander's Palace (jazz)

Court of Two Sisters (jazz)
Gulfstream St. Charles (jazz)
Hard Rock Cafe (varies)
Impastato's (vocals)
Irene's Cuisine (piano)
Jamila's Cafe (varies)
Landry's Seafood (varies)
La Provence (piano)
La Thai (guitar)
Marigny Brasserie (jazz)
Mulate's (Cajun)
Muriel's Jackson Sq. (jazz)
One Restaurant (Latin)
Palace Café (jazz)
Parkway Bakery (varies)
Pelican Club (piano)
Ralph's on Park (piano)
Rib Room (jazz)
Saltwater Grill (jazz band)
Tommy's Cuisine (piano)
Tony Mandina's (piano)

Family-Style
Anselmo's
Azul
Bank Cafe
Brick Oven Cafe
Bubba Gump
Byblos
Cuco's
Dong Phuong
Don's Seafood
Fausto's Bistro
Fury's
Great Wall
Jack Dempsey's
Jamila's Cafe
Kim Son
Mosca's
Mother's
New Orleans Food
P.F. Chang's
Royal China
Shogun
Siamese
Sun Ray Grill
Two Tony's

Fireplaces

Andrea's
Court of Two Sisters
Crystal Room
Jackson
La Provence
Le Citron Bistro
Louisiana Pizza
Rest. des Familles
Stella!
Table One

Game in Season

Andrea's
August
Bacco
Bank Cafe
Brigtsen's
Cafe Atchafalaya
Commander's Palace
Cuvée
Dakota, The
Dick & Jenny's
Emeril's Delmonico
Irene's Cuisine
Iris
La Petite Grocery
La Provence
Longbranch, The
Madrid
Marigny Brasserie
Mat & Naddie's
New Orleans Grill
Olivier's
Upperline

Historic Places

(Year opened; * building)
1795 Feelings Cafe*
1795 Gumbo Shop*
1797 Napoleon House*
1810 Le Citron Bistro*
1834 La Louisiane*
1839 Oak Alley*
1840 Antoine's
1853 Begue's
1856 Tujague's

1862 Café Du Monde
1870 Morning Call
1877 Upperline*
1880 Commander's Palace
1890 La Petite Grocery*
1890 Longbranch, The*
1890 Sun Ray Grill*
1893 Whole Foods*
1894 Coffee Pot*
1900 Mat & Naddie's*
1902 Ernst Cafe*
1905 Angelo Brocato
1905 Galatoire's
1906 Central Grocery
1907 Crystal Room
1910 Acme Oyster
1913 Pascal's Manale
1916 Liuzza's by Track
1918 Arnaud's
1919 Casamento's*
1920 Broussard's
1920 Nardo's Trattoria*
1924 Domilise's
1928 Bozo's
1929 Ye Olde College Inn*
1930 Court of Two Sisters
1931 St. Charles Tavern
1934 Middendorf's
1937 Fiorella's Café
1937 Nuvolari's*
1938 Mother's
1939 Hansen's Sno-Bliz
1942 Franky & Johnny's
1946 Brennan's
1946 Mosca's
1947 Liuzza's Restaurant
1950 Clover Grill
1952 Parasol's
1953 Bon Ton Café

Hotel Dining

Astor Crowne Plaza Hotel
   Bourbon House
Baronne Plaza Hotel
   Streetcar Bistro
Garden District Hotel
   Vizard's on the Ave.

Restaurant Special Features

Harrah's Hotel
  Riche
Hotel InterContinental
  Veranda
Hotel Le Cirque
  Mike's on the Ave.
Hôtel Provincial
  Stella!
JW Marriott
  Shula's
Lafayette Hotel
  Anatole
Le Pavillon Hotel
  Crystal Room
Loews New Orleans Hotel
  Café Adelaide
Maison Dupuy Hotel
  Dominique's
New Orleans Marriott at the
  Convention Ctr.
  Wolfe's in Warehouse
Omni Royal Orleans
  Rib Room
Renaissance Arts Hotel
  La Côte Brasserie
Riverfront Hotel
  7 on Fulton
Royal Sonesta Hotel
  Begue's
Windsor Court Hotel
  New Orleans Grill
W New Orleans
  Bacco
  Zoë

Late Dining

(Weekday closing hour)
Angeli on Decatur (2 AM)
Beachcorner B&G (1 AM)
Bud's Broiler (24 hrs.)
Café Du Monde (24 hrs.)
Cafe Roma (12 AM)
Clover Grill (24 hrs.)
Coop's Place (2 AM)
Delachaise, The (2 AM)
Ernst Cafe (12 AM)
Morning Call (24 hrs.)

O'Henry's (12 AM)
Port of Call (12 AM)
rue de la course (12 AM)
St. Charles Tavern (24 hrs.)
13 Monaghan (4 AM)

Local Favorites

Alberta
Bon Ton Café
Bozo's
Byblos
Café Degas
Cafe Rani
Crabby Jack's
Croissant d'Or
Dante's Kitchen
Deanie's Seafood
Drago's
Elizabeth's
Hansen's Sno-Bliz
Jack Dempsey's
Jacques-Imo's
K-Paul's
Liuzza's by Track
Liuzza's Restaurant
Martinique Bistro
Middendorf's
Napoleon House
Petunia's
R & O's
Ye Olde College Inn

Meet for a Drink

Abita Brew Pub
Arnaud's
Crescent City Brew
Ernst Cafe
Gordon Biersch
GW Fins
Herbsaint
Houston's
Muriel's Jackson Sq.
Pelican Club
Red Fish Grill

Noteworthy Newcomers

Alberta
Anatole

Azul
Calas Bistro
Civello's
Cochon
Coffea Gallery
Eat
Fiesta Bistro
Gulfstream St. Charles
Ignatius Eatery
Iris
Jackson
Jazz Tacos
La Boca
Longbranch, The
Melting Pot
Mike's on the Ave.
Minnie's Catfish
Riche
7 on Fulton
Shula's
Table One
Vizard's on the Ave.
Wolfe's in Warehouse

Offbeat
Adolfo's
Byblos
Café Degas
Central Grocery
Civello's
Coffea Gallery
Country Flame
Delachaise, The
Dick & Jenny's
Eleven 79
Fausto's Bistro
Home Furnishings
Jacques-Imo's
Le Citron Bistro
Mat & Naddie's
Mother's
Parasol's
Port of Call
Praline Connection
Savvy Gourmet
Slim Goodies

Outdoor Dining
(G=garden; P=patio;
S=sidewalk; T=terrace)
Abita Brew Pub (G,P)
Alpine, The (G)
Audubon Park (T)
Babylon Café (S)
Basil Leaf (S)
Bayona (P)
Beachcorner B&G (P)
Brennan's (G)
Brick Oven Cafe (P)
Broussard's (P)
Bubba Gump (P,T)
Bywater BBQ (P)
Cafe Atchafalaya (S)
Cafe Beignet (P)
Café Du Monde (P)
Cafe Rani (P)
Caffe! Caffe! (P,S)
Calas Bistro (P)
Carreta's Grill (P)
CC's Coffee (P)
Chateau Coffee (S)
Coffea Gallery (G)
Coffee Cottage (S)
Coffee Pot (P)
Coffee Rani (P,S)
Commander's Palace (P)
Court of Two Sisters (P)
Crazy Johnnie's (T)
Crescent City Brew (P,T)
Croissant d'Or (P)
Cuco's (P)
Dante's Kitchen (P)
Dick & Jenny's (P)
Dominique's (P)
Feelings Cafe (P)
Fellini's (S)
Fire (P)
Flaming Torch (S)
Fresco Cafe (T)
Galley (P)
GB's Patio B&G (P)
Gordon Biersch (P)
Gumbo Shop (P)
Hard Rock Cafe (T)

Restaurant Special Features

Herbsaint (S)
Ignatius Eatery (S)
Iris (T)
Jackson (T)
Jacques-Imo's (P)
Jamila's Cafe (T)
Jazmine Café (P)
Jazz Tacos (S)
Joint, The (G,S)
K-Paul's (T)
La Boulangerie (S)
La Crêpe Nanou (S)
La Madeleine (P,S)
Lebanon's Café (P)
Le Citron Bistro (P)
Le Parvenu (P)
Lilette (P)
Louisiana Pizza (S)
Lucy's (S)
Maple St. Cafe (P)
Martinique Bistro (G,P)
Martin Wine Cellar (P)
Mat & Naddie's (P)
Minnie's Catfish (P)
Mona's Cafe (P,S)
Nacho Mama's (P)
Napoleon House (P)
New Orleans Food (P)
New York Pizza (S)
Nirvana Indian (P)
Oak Alley (P)
O'Henry's (S,T)
Parkway Bakery (P)
Pelican Club (S)
PJ's Coffee (P)
Ralph's on Park (T)
Rock-n-Sake (S)
Roly Poly (S)
Royal Blend (G,P)
rue de la course (S)
Russell's Marina (P)
Saltwater Grill (P)
Schiro's (P)
Semolina Pasta (P,T)
Serrano's Salsa (P)
Slice (S)
Slim Goodies (G)

Stella! (P)
Sun Ray Grill (P)
Superior Grill (P)
Table One (S)
Taqueria Corona (S)
Theo's (S)
Ugly Dog Saloon (P)
Vizard's on the Ave. (P)
Voodoo BBQ (P)
Whole Foods (P)

Parking
(V=valet, *=validated)
Bacco*
Bayona*
Begue's (V)*
Besh Steak*
Bon Ton Café*
Brennan's*
Café Adelaide (V)
Cochon*
Commander's Palace (V)
Cuvée (V)
Dickie Brennan's (V)*
Dominique's (V)*
Emeril's (V)
Emeril's Delmonico (V)
Gordon Biersch*
GW Fins*
Herbsaint (V)
K-Paul's*
La Côte Brasserie (V)
La Louisiane*
Laurentino's Tapas*
Morton's*
Mr. John's (V)
Muriel's Jackson Sq.*
New Orleans Grill (V)*
Palace Café*
Pelican Club*
Peristyle (V)
Ralph's on Park (V)
Rib Room*
RioMar*
Ruth's Chris (V)
Semolina Pasta (V)
7 on Fulton (V)

Shula's (V)
Stella! (V)
Veranda (V)
Vizard's on the Ave. (V)
Wolfe's in Warehouse (V)
Zea (V)
Zoë (V)

People-Watching
Antoine's
Arnaud's
Bacco
Bank Cafe
Bayona
Brennan's
Brigtsen's
Café Adelaide
Café Du Monde
Café East
Cafe Maspero
Cafe Pontalba
Clancy's
Clover Grill
Coffee Pot
Commander's Palace
Country Flame
Delachaise, The
Dickie Brennan's
Emeril's
Emeril's Delmonico
Galatoire's
Gumbo Shop
Irene's Cuisine
K-Paul's
La Crêpe Nanou
La Louisiane
La Petite Grocery
Le Parvenu
Liborio Cuban
Mother's
Muriel's Jackson Sq.
New Orleans Grill
NOLA
Palace Café
Parasol's
Pelican Club
Peristyle

Ralph's on Park
Rib Room
Ruth's Chris
Taqueros
Tommy's Cuisine
Trey Yuen
Upperline
Veranda
Vizard's on the Ave.

Power Scenes
Andrea's
Antoine's
Arnaud's
August
Brennan's
Café Adelaide
Commander's Palace
Emeril's
Emeril's Delmonico
Galatoire's
La Petite Grocery
New Orleans Grill
Peristyle
Ralph's on Park
Rib Room
Ruth's Chris
Veranda

Prix Fixe Menus
(Call for prices and times)
Acropolis
Arnaud's
Bank Cafe
Bayona
Brennan's
Broussard's
Cafe Giovanni
Carmine's
Court of Two Sisters
Cuvée
Emeril's
Five Happiness
Gumbo Shop
Impastato's
Jackson
La Crêpe Nanou

Restaurant Special Features

La Provence
La Thai
Martinique Bistro
NOLA
Palace Café
Petunia's
Rest. des Familles
Rib Room
RioMar
Sake Cafe
7 on Fulton
Stella!
Tujague's
Upperline
Vega Tapas
Vizard's on the Ave.

Quick Bites
(Besides fast food and diners)
Adolfo's
Angeli on Decatur
Apple Seed
Audubon Park
Babylon Café
Beachcorner B&G
Coffee Pot
Crabby Jack's
Crazy Johnnie's
DiMartino's
Fiorella's Café
Joey K's
Marigny Brasserie
Martin Wine Cellar
Oscar's
Parasol's

Quiet Conversation
Alberta
Antoine's
Broussard's
Byblos
Cafe Giovanni
Cuvée
Feelings Cafe
Flaming Torch
Horinoya
La Côte Brasserie

La Provence
Le Parvenu
Mimi's
New Orleans Grill
Streetcar Bistro
Taj Mahal
Zoë

Raw Bars
Acme Oyster
Bourbon House
Bozo's
Casamento's
Deanie's Seafood
Don's Seafood
Drago's
Harbor Seafood
Landry's Seafood
Pascal's Manale
Red Fish Grill
Remoulade
Saltwater Grill
Zeke's

Romantic Places
Andrea's
Antoine's
Arnaud's
August
Bacco
Bayona
Brennan's
Broussard's
Cafe Giovanni
Commander's Palace
Crystal Room
Cuvée
Emeril's
Emeril's Delmonico
Feelings Cafe
Irene's Cuisine
Iris
La Crêpe Nanou
La Provence
Lilette
New Orleans Grill
Rib Room

Sara's
Stella!
Upperline

Senior Appeal
Anselmo's
Betsy's Pancake
Bon Ton Café
Bozo's
Bravo! Cucina
Brick Oven Cafe
Cafe DiBlasi
Cannon's
Casamento's
Chateau Coffee
Drago's
Fausto's Bistro
Fury's
Great Wall
Gumbo Shop
Impastato's
Jack Dempsey's
Joey K's
Kosher Cajun Deli
La Louisiane
La Provence
Mr. John's
New Orleans Hamburger
Riccobono's Peppermill
Russell's Marina
Saltwater Grill
Semolina Pasta
Vincent's
Ye Olde College Inn

Singles Scenes
Abita Brew Pub
Acme Oyster
Cafe Atchafalaya
Café East
Cafe Maspero
Cafe Rani
Eleven 79
Ernst Cafe
Franky & Johnny's
GB's Patio B&G
Gumbo Shop

Hana Japanese
Kyoto
Lola's
Louisiana Pizza
Lucy's
Mat & Naddie's
Morning Call
Napoleon House
Parasol's
Port of Call
Reginelli's
Remoulade
Rock-n-Sake
Royal Blend
Semolina Pasta
Semolina's Bistro
Slim Goodies
Superior Grill
13 Monaghan
Ugly Dog Saloon
Zea

Sleepers
(Good to excellent food,
but little known)
Caffe! Caffe!
Calas Bistro
Casablanca
Chateau du Lac
Civello's
Clementine's
Coffee Rani
Coop's Place
DiMartino's
Dominique's
Etoile
Frosty's Café
Hillbilly BBQ
Horinoya
Jamila's Cafe
La Provence
Laurentino's Tapas
Longbranch, The
Mark Twain's Pizza
Mr. John's
Nuvolari's
Olivier's

Pho Bang
Rest. des Familles
Ristorante Da Piero
Ristorante Filippo
Royal China
Sal & Judy's
Sara's
Siamese
Singha
Sugar Park Tavern
Tan Dinh
Tony Mandina's
Two Tony's
Young's

Special Occasions

Antoine's
Arnaud's
August
Bayona
Café Adelaide
Commander's Palace
Cuvée
Emeril's
Galatoire's
New Orleans Grill
Ralph's on Park
Stella!
Upperline

Takeout

Andrea's
Angelo Brocato
Bank Cafe
Bozo's
Brigtsen's
Byblos
Bywater BBQ
Café Degas
Café Du Monde
Cafe Rani
Cafe Roma
Carreta's Grill
Casamento's
Central Grocery
Coffee Cottage
Coffee Rani

Copeland's
Corky's BBQ
Croissant d'Or
Dante's Kitchen
Deanie's Seafood
DiMartino's
Domilise's
Fellini's
Five Happiness
Franky & Johnny's
Fury's
Galley
Italian Pie
Jacques-Imo's
Joey K's
Joint, The
Juan's Flying Burrito
La Boulangerie
La Madeleine
Lee's Hamburgers
Liborio Cuban
Liuzza's by Track
Louisiana Pizza
Lucy's
Mark Twain's Pizza
Martin Wine Cellar
Mat & Naddie's
Mona's Cafe
Mother's
Mr. Ed's
New Orleans Food
New Orleans Hamburger
New York Pizza
Nine Roses
NINJA
Nirvana Indian
Nuvolari's
O'Henry's
P.F. Chang's
PJ's Coffee
Popeyes
Port of Call
Praline Connection
R & O's
Roly Poly
Royal Blend
Russell's Marina

Saltwater Grill
Savvy Gourmet
Semolina Pasta
Slice
Slim Goodies
Smilie's
Sun Ray Grill
Taqueria Corona
Theo's
Trolley Stop Cafe
Voodoo BBQ
Whole Foods
Ye Olde College Inn
Zea

Teen Appeal
Bozo's
Bravo! Cucina
Cafe Roma
Cannon's
Coffee Rani
Cuco's
Domilise's
Franky & Johnny's
Hana Japanese
Harbor Seafood
Hard Rock Cafe
Houston's
Jacques-Imo's
Jamila's Cafe
Jazmine Café
Juan's Flying Burrito
Kyoto
Louisiana Pizza
Mark Twain's Pizza
Mat & Naddie's
Mona Lisa
New York Pizza
NINJA
O'Henry's
R & O's
Reginelli's
Remoulade
Royal Blend
Russell's Marina
Semolina Pasta
Semolina's Bistro

Shogun
Sun Ray Grill
Superior Grill
Taqueria Corona
Trolley Stop Cafe
Zea

Trendy
Alberta
Bacco
Bank Cafe
Bayona
Brennan's
Brigtsen's
Café East
Cafe Maspero
Clancy's
Commander's Palace
Cuvée
Dante's Kitchen
Dick & Jenny's
Domilise's
Eleven 79
Emeril's
Feelings Cafe
Galatoire's
Gordon Biersch
Herbsaint
Kyoto
La Crêpe Nanou
La Petite Grocery
Lilette
Mat & Naddie's
New Orleans Grill
NINJA
NOLA
Palace Café
Pelican Club
Peristyle
Red Fish Grill
Rock-n-Sake
Ruth's Chris
Sake Cafe
Savvy Gourmet
Table One
Taqueros
13 Monaghan

Upperline
Vega Tapas
Vizard's on the Ave.

Views
Anatole
Audubon Park
Brothers Sushi
Cafe Pontalba
Commander's Palace
K-Paul's
Louisiana Pizza
Muriel's Jackson Sq.
Oak Alley
Parkway Bakery
Ralph's on Park
Rest. des Familles
Superior Grill
Trey Yuen

Visitors on Expense Account
Antoine's
Arnaud's
August
Bacco
Brennan's
Broussard's
Commander's Palace
Emeril's
Emeril's Delmonico
Galatoire's
La Provence
New Orleans Grill
Palace Café
Pascal's Manale
Pelican Club
Peristyle
Rib Room
Ruth's Chris
7 on Fulton

Winning Wine Lists
Antoine's
Arnaud's
Bacco
Bayona
Brennan's
Brigtsen's
Café Adelaide
Clancy's
Commander's Palace
Cuvée
Emeril's
Martin Wine Cellar
New Orleans Grill
Peristyle

Worth a Trip
Abita Springs
   Abita Brew Pub
   Longbranch, The
Avondale
   Mosca's
Covington
   Dakota, The
   Etoile
Crown Point
   Rest. des Familles
Hammond
   Trey Yuen
Kenner
   Le Parvenu
Lacombe
   La Provence
   Sal & Judy's
Manchac
   Middendorf's
Mandeville
   Nuvolari's
   Trey Yuen

Nightlife

Most Popular

Most Popular

Each surveyor has been asked to name his or her five favorite places. This list reflects their choices.

1. Pat O'Brien's
2. House of Blues
3. Tipitina's
4. Preservation Hall
5. Columns Hotel
6. Lafitte's Blacksmith*
7. Jimmy Buffett's
8. Mid-City Lanes
9. Maple Leaf
10. Snug Harbor Jazz
11. Bourbon Pub/Parade
12. Cat's Meow
13. Bombay Club
14. Bulldog, The
15. Carousel Bar
16. Old Absinthe Hse.
17. St. Joe's Bar
18. Razzoo Bar & Patio
19. Oz
20. Cafe Lafitte in Exile
21. Molly's at Market
22. d.b.a.
23. Famous Door
24. Kingpin
25. Whiskey Blue
26. Cooter Brown's
27. Bourbon St. Blues
28. Coyote Ugly*
29. Le Bon Temps Roulé
30. F&M Patio Bar
31. Le Chat Noir
32. Snake & Jake's*
33. Gold Mine Saloon
34. Mayfair, The
35. Fritzel's Jazz
36. Dos Jefes Cigar
37. Spotted Cat
38. Swizzle Stick*
39. Circle Bar
40. Cajun Cabin
41. Maison Jazz*
42. Bruno's
43. Monkey Hill*
44. One Eyed Jacks*
45. Tropical Isle*
46. Howlin' Wolf

It should go without saying that New Orleans is famous for its nightlife. Though a few popular bars and clubs can be pricey, budget-conscious nightcrawlers will have no trouble finding what they seek here. To help them, we have included a list of the Best Buys at the bottom of page 114.

---

* Indicates a tie with place above

Top Rated Nightlife Spots

Excluding places with low voting.

Appeal

27 Maple Leaf	Snug Harbor Jazz
Mid-City Lanes	Le Chat Noir
Tipitina's	Pat O'Brien's
26 Vaughan's Lounge	Columns Hotel
Preservation Hall	**25** Carousel Bar

Decor

27 Loa
26 Columns Hotel
Swizzle Stick
25 Hookah Café
Carousel Bar
24 Whiskey Blue
Bombay Club
23 St. Joe's Bar
House of Blues
One Eyed Jacks

Service

24 Rawhide 2010
Milan Lounge
Bourbon Pub/Parade
Swizzle Stick
Molly's at Market
Cafe Lafitte in Exile
23 Loa
Carousel Bar
Mayfair, The
Le Chat Noir

By Category

Listed in order of Appeal rating

Cocktail Experts

25 Carousel Bar
24 Loa
Swizzle Stick
St. Joe's Bar
22 Bridge Lounge

Hotel Bars

26 Columns Hotel
25 Carousel Bar
24 Loa
Swizzle Stick
23 Whiskey Blue

Dance Clubs

24 Bourbon Pub/Parade
One Eyed Jacks
22 Dungeon, The
Republic New Orleans
21 Oz

Jazz Clubs

26 Vaughan's Lounge
Preservation Hall
Snug Harbor Jazz
25 Fritzel's Jazz
23 Donna's B&G

Dives

27 Maple Leaf
26 Vaughan's Lounge
24 Molly's at Market
Circle Bar
23 Mayfair, The

Local Favorites

27 Maple Leaf
Mid-City Lanes
Tipitina's
26 Vaughan's Lounge
Snug Harbor Jazz

Best Buys

1. Ms. Mae's	6. Rawhide 2010
2. Milan Lounge	7. Rivershack Tavern
3. Bruno's	8. Snake & Jake's
4. St. Joe's Bar	9. Cafe Lafitte in Exile
5. Vaughan's Lounge	10. Maple Leaf

Ratings & Symbols

Credit Cards: ⌀ no credit cards accepted

Ratings are on a scale of **0** to **30**.

| A | Appeal | D | Decor | S | Service |

▽ low response/less reliable

Cost ($) reflects our surveyors' estimate of the price of an average drink.

For places listed without ratings, the price range is:

| I | Inexpensive (below $5) | E | Expensive ($9 to $11) |
| M | Moderate ($5 to $8) | VE | Very Expensive ($11+) |

| A | D | S | C |

Abbey, The ⌀ | 18 | 14 | 19 | $5 |
1123 Decatur St. (bet. Governor Nicholls St. & Ursuline Ave.), 504-523-7177
"Debauchery" comes free with the cheap, stiff drinks at this dark, "open-all-night" French Quarter "dive", along with "entertaining" live jazz and hip-hop DJs; some warn not to "look too closely at the floors", but fans keep flocking "because it's a scene" of "service industry folk" among other tattooed and pierced habitués.

Applebarrel ⌀ | 19 | 14 | 17 | $5 |
609 Frenchmen St. (Chartres St.), 504-949-9399
The "music sizzles" when "lesser-known but top-notch" local blues acts, and even "washboard bands", play this Marigny "hole-in-the-wall" that serves "affordable drinks"; it's "packed if 10 people are in the room", and among the "aging hippies, barflies, tourists and young hipsters" are always a few true "New Orleans characters" who'll give you "a story to tell" the next morning.

Avenue Pub | 14 | 9 | 22 | $5 |
1732 St. Charles Ave. (bet. Euterpe & Polymnia Sts.), 504-586-9243
An "excellent staff" turns this "decent" 24-hour "dive bar" in the Lower Garden District into a "friendly" place for late-night eats – "as long as you love grease"; during Mardi Gras, it's the ideal place to "catch the parades", though some don't see the appeal "any other time of year."

Balcony Bar, The | 20 | 14 | 17 | $5 |
3201 Magazine St. (Harmony St.), 504-895-1600
Twentysomethings and Tulaners hang out on the "mellow" upstairs balcony to "watch the sunset on Magazine

Street" or else socialize with the "quirky people playing pool" in the "dumpy" downstairs of this "chill" "college bar"; there's also a solid pub-grub menu, served until 4 AM ("always a good thing when you're drinking").

Banks Street Bar & Grill ⊄ ▽ 20 13 19 $4
4401 Banks St. (Alexander St.), 504-486-0258;
www.banksstreetbar.com
This "little neighborhood bar" with a "solely local" Mid-City clientele "hung tough after Katrina", quickly re-opening in a heavily flooded zone and still booking free music shows nightly; it's "pretty much a dive, but chill and relaxing" nonetheless with "tables outside for lounging" and complimentary red beans and rice on Mondays.

Big Top Gallery – – – M
1638 Clio St. (bet. Carondelet St. & St. Charles Ave.), 504-569-2700;
www.3rcp.com
"Hip, funky and arty", this "gallery meets performance space meets bar" hosts "odd and eclectic" acts that range from spoken word performances to avant-garde jazz; the Lower Garden District neighborhood can be a "little shady", but the "bohos" keep coming back for the "great vibe" and the "locals-only art scene."

Bombay Club 25 24 21 $11
830 Conti St. (bet. Bourbon & Dauphine Sts.), 504-586-0972;
www.thebombayclub.com
"An adult oasis" off Bourbon Street, this "romantic" hotel bar with "overstuffed leather chairs" provides a "quaint little getaway" from the "crush of the Quarter"; its clientele indulges in of "Creole-inspired comfort food" and "pricey" "well-made martinis" from a list "longer than the Great Wall", as crooners and jazz musicians play "slinky" tunes.

Boot, The 11 7 10 $4
1039 Broadway (Zimpel St.), 504-866-9008
"Underclassmen run rampant" at this Uptown magnet for "wild crowds" of Tulane students who need "somewhere to party besides the dorm room"; while most voters avoid this "kiddie zone", often nicknamed "Drinking 101", a few like to "watch the game" with rounds of "cheap beer" and "reminisce about those bygone college days."

Bourbon Pub/Parade ⊄ 24 19 24 $6
801 Bourbon St. (St. Ann St.), 504-529-2107;
www.bourbonpub.com
"Ground zero for gay nightlife" in the French Quarter, this "raucous" club hosts "a big crowd" that congregates to watch videos in the "airy" downstairs, while "hot boys" "steam up" the upper-level with their "bumping and grinding"; guests exude "just the right amount of attitude" and the "friendly" bartenders welcome those of all "persuasions", but "dress to impress or go home alone."

Bourbon Street Blues Company | 22 | | 16 | | 18 | | $10 |
441 Bourbon St. (St. Louis St.), 504-566-1507
Fans of this French Quarter venue get "sucked in" by the
cover bands playing classic rock, soul and blues – "you'll
hear the music from half a block away" – as well as by the
chance to hang out "on a balcony over Bourbon" ("bring
some beads"); some grouse that it "could be anywhere in
America" ("cheesy, cheesy, cheesy"), but others prize the
"local secret" of three-for-one drinks upstairs.

Bridge Lounge | 22 | | 20 | | 19 | | $6 |
1201 Magazine St. (Erato St.), 504-299-1888;
www.bridgelounge.com
"Patrons of the four-legged variety" frolic at this pooch-
friendly Lower Garden District "neighborhood bar" decorated with "adorable photos of dogs"; it "looks like a
shack" from the outside, but inside "grad students and
young professionals" lounge in the "low-key", "candlelit
room" over "wine flights" and "great mojitos."

Bruno's | 19 | | 16 | | 19 | | $4 |
7538 Maple St. (Hillary St.), 504-861-7615 **NEW**
7601 Maple St. (Hillary St.), 504-861-7615
www.brunosbar.com
"A hell of a hullabaloo" awaits at this Uptown sports bar
"catering to the college crowd" with "a pool table, patio,
darts and daily drink specials", and accommodating "their
grandfathers" on the earlier side; a fixture since the '50s, it
recently expanded with a second indoor/outdoor branch
across the street (7538 Maple) that has "no soul yet", but
features plenty of flat-screen TVs, shuffleboard and a
burger-centric kitchen (serving both locales).

Bulldog, The | 23 | | 18 | | 20 | | $5 |
5135 Canal Blvd. (City Park Ave.), 504-488-4191
3236 Magazine St. (bet. Pleasant & Toledo Sts.), 504-891-1516
www.draftfreak.com
It's "all about the beer" at this Uptown and Mid-City duo
where a "mostly under-30 crowd" "chums it up and blows
off some steam" while quaffing brews from a 150-strong
selection (sample all 50 drafts and "get your name on a
plaque"); while both locales also have patios in common,
as well as "free pint glasses" on Wednesdays, the
Magazine Street branch appeals to "prepsters" and Canal
Street has neighborhood devotees who praise its quick re-
opening post-Katrina for "the few folks that were back."

Café Brasil ⌐ | 23 | | 15 | | 16 | | $6 |
2100 Chartres St. (Frenchmen St.), unlisted phone
"Fantastic lineups" get the crowd "bumping" at this "hot"
Marigny dance club, which attracts "old Latino men happy
to dance the night away" and "beautiful people truly enjoying themselves" (especially late) with "a little sensual

sweating to Latin rhythms"; some complain about the un-predictable schedule and "no-frills room", but "you don't go there because it looks good", you go for the "Caribbean street festival" vibe.

Cafe Lafitte in Exile　　23 | 19 | 24 | $5 |
901 Bourbon St. (Dumaine St.), 504-522-8397; www.lafittes.com
"Cruise, see and be seen" at this "terrific" French Quarter "staple" – reputedly the city's "oldest gay bar" – where the "friendliest staff" and "uninhibited patrons" keep things hopping 24/7; if partisans affectionately dis the joint as "our dump", it's the perfect setting for Sunday's 'Trash Disco' party, the "best way to cap off a weekend."

Cajun Cabin　　　　20 | 18 | 18 | $12 |
501 Bourbon St. (St. Louis St.), 504-529-4256;
www.cajuncabin.com
"Cajun music, cold beer and crawfish – any questions?" demand zydeco zealots who patronize this venue with "great bands" nightly; you can dance, "have a few drinks and some grub" and "even strap on the washboard, use your spoon and play along" if so inspired; the Bourbon Street locale means you'll probably "see lots of tourists", but "great memories" are made here nonetheless.

Carousel Bar　　　　25 | 25 | 23 | $9 |
Hotel Monteleone, 214 Royal St. (bet. Bienville Ave. & Iberville St.), 504-523-3341
"The room spins even before you order your first drink" at this revolving, brightly decorated "merry-go-round" cock-tail lounge overlooking the Quarter from the "historic" Hotel Monteleone; its live piano music, "genteel", "grown-up atmosphere" and "carousel of characters" add up to an "old-liner" that "out-of-towners love."

Carrollton Station　　　21 | 15 | 18 | $5 |
8140 Willow St. (Dublin St.), 504-865-9190;
www.carrolltonstation.com
Carrollton-dwellers "escape the college scene" at this "cool neighborhood hangout" housed in a nearly century-old building, which proffers "cheap drinks" from a "won-derful old Victorian mahogany bar"; the "intimate" stage often showcases local singer-songwriters, but the space – which once hid a brothel – also holds "enough cubbyholes to sneak away for a quiet talk."

Cat's Meow　　　　　21 | 14 | 16 | $8 |
701 Bourbon St. (St. Peter St.), 504-523-2788;
www.catsmeow-neworleans.com
"Calling all *American Idol* wannabes" – step onstage at this "karaoke kingdom on Bourbon Street", where the "MCs do a great job getting people to participate" and the "loud and rowdy" crowd "howls with the singing custom-ers"; "packed to the gills" with "drunken tourists" who

spill onto the balcony for people-watching, it's "cheap", "cheesy" and "hard to get a drink at the bar", but when you're raring to go it "rocks."

Checkpoint Charlie's   17 | 13 | 20 | $6
501 Esplanade Ave. (Decatur St.), 504-281-4847
A "crossroads for all kinds", this "combination bar, grill and Laundromat" on the Quarter's edge boasts live music nightly and a staff that "really scrambles to keep the food and drink flowing"; since it's open 24 hours, "you can always find a drinking partner" or pool buddy, have a burger and wash your whites, though "that's a little ambitious at 6 AM."

Chickie Wah Wah NEW   – | – | – | M
2828 Canal St. (S. White St.), 504-304-4714;
www.chickiewahwah.com
In a section of Mid-City that saw deep water after Katrina and little activity since, this new club is a beacon of blues, funk and rock 'n' roll that attracts local music luminaries as both headliners and unannounced guests; signs from defunct nightspots line the narrow room with a pool table, jukebox and a long bar.

Circle Bar ▱   24 | 20 | 20 | $6
1032 St. Charles Ave. (Lee Circle), 504-588-2616
"The hip crowd" grooves to "obscure acts" and "old R&B artists from days gone by" at this "little place for those in-the-know" on Lee Circle; with "red walls", "dim lights" and a riverboat mural above the bar, it has a "retro feel" that's clinched by the massive purple K&B drugstore clock hanging from the ceiling.

COLUMNS HOTEL BAR   26 | 26 | 20 | $7
Columns Hotel, 3811 St. Charles Ave. (bet. General Taylor & Peniston Sts.), 504-899-9308; www.thecolumns.com
Suited to "sunset cocktails with Scarlet O'Hara", this "beautiful Victorian hotel" in the Garden District evokes "a different era", as guests "sit on the front porch sipping mint juleps" mixed by "knowledgeable bartenders" and soak in the "St. Charles charm"; its equally impressive, "exquisite" interior hosts live jazz, Cajun and piano tunes, and "everyone eventually strolls through" – whether in "shorts or a ball gown."

Cooter Brown's Tavern   21 | 17 | 19 | $5
509 S. Carrollton Ave. (St. Charles Ave.), 504-866-9104;
www.cooterbrowns.com
"Zillions" of "exotic bottles and drafts" and "fresh-shucked oysters" served "as cold as the brews" win hearts at this "loud" Carrollton neighborhood "sports bar" and "suds lover's paradise"; pool tables and satellite links to pro games distract from the "purely functional" decor of "long picnic tables" and "caricature carvings" but, says one reviewer, "beer and plasma TV – a man needs no more."

Corner Pocket ⌂

20   13   21 $5

940 St. Louis St. (Burgundy St.), 504-568-9829;
www.cornerpocket.net

"Walk on the wild side" at this French Quarter "gay dive"
where "below-standard strippers" (aka "twinks" "in biki-
nis") strut their stuff on the bar; the crowd can be "surly", but
"good drinks" and "service with a smile (and then some)"
lend it a "certain charm"; wannabes can shed their
inhibitions – and clothes – at Friday's 'New Meat' contest.

Coyote Ugly

14   13   16 $10

225 N. Peters St. (Iberville St.), 504-561-0003;
www.coyoteuglysaloon.com

"Hot chick bartenders" sporting skimpy tops, cowboy hats
and "attitude" rule this "rowdy" French Quarter chain link
known for "great body shots"; while the "tacky" "sausage-
fest" atmosphere is not everyone's "cup of T and A", the
hormone-charged swear you "can't beat the girls dancing
on the bar" – though females who find it "tough to get service" probably wish they could.

d.b.a.

24   20   19 $7

618 Frenchmen St. (bet. Chartres & Royal Sts.), 504-942-3731;
www.drinkgoodstuff.com

"Great local jazz and rock" draws an "interesting mix" to
this "hard-to-beat" Marigny "hangout" where window-
front "cubbyholes" and "cool red lighting" create an "intimate", "funky" atmosphere; an "impressive offering of imported beer", scotch and other "top-notch" "liquid
pleasures" wows connoisseurs, who proclaim the "hidden
treasure" "better than the NYC" original (but admit it's "a
little pricey for New Orleans").

Donna's Bar & Grill

23   11   19 $8

800 N. Rampart St. (St. Ann St.), 504-596-6914;
www.donnasbarandgrill.com

"Funky" live acts are the draw at this "monument to brass
bands" and traditional jazz on an "iffy" edge of the French
Quarter where "tourists seldom stumble"; a "typical New
Orleans" "dive", it's known "not for its decor" but for its
"friendly" vibe, "wonderful music" and "free red beans
and rice" on Monday nights; N.B. open for lunch weekdays, but at night Saturday–Monday only.

Dos Jefes Uptown Cigar Bar

22   20   20 $7

5535 Tchoupitoulas St. (Joseph St.), 504-891-8500

There's "never a bad gig" at this "dark, cozy" jazz and cigar bar "a little off the beaten path" Uptown; its "great
whiskey selection" is equaled by the "wide array of sto-
gies", which is a boon to aficionados but a bane to those
who "could do without" the "heavy smoke" – though
there's always fresh air on the "sweet patio" bar "lined
with porch swings."

Dragon's Den
| _ | _ | _ | I |

435 Esplanade Ave. (Frenchmen St.), 504-949-1750

Down a narrow alley and up a winding flight of stairs, this shadowy red lair, a destination for cutting-edge noise and offbeat acts in the Marigny, could be an opium den gone legit; performances on the small center stage range from belly dancing to off-kilter avant-garde klezmer, and there's a balcony to take a breather from the heady room.

Dungeon, The
| 22 | 19 | 19 | $8 |

738 Toulouse St. (Bourbon St.), 504-523-5530;
www.originaldungeon.com

It's "Marilyn Manson meets Bourbon Street" at this "kinky" and "creepy underground" French Quarter warren that's "smaller than an NYC apartment" and populated by "vampire girls", "headbangers" and the occasional conventioneer; order a signature Dragon's Blood cocktail and follow the "narrow hallways" upstairs where "throbbing industrial, new wave, Goth and rock 'n' roll are on constant rotation."

Famous Door
| 21 | 13 | 17 | $9 |

339 Bourbon St. (Bienville St.), 504-598-4334

"Party purists" groove to "Top 40" cover bands at this "wild, crowded" French Quarter spot where "fun is the objective" and the "music never stops"; for better or worse, it's the bar you "imagine whenever you think of Bourbon Street", a "classic" with "lots of history" – though cynics snipe that over the years it's become more like "the other touristy dives" nearby.

F&M Patio Bar
| 21 | 11 | 16 | $4 |

4841 Tchoupitoulas St. (Lyons St.), 504-895-6784

"Don't even think of arriving until midnight" at this "gritty" Uptown "favorite", a "last call" "local joint" bursting with "drunk" college kids "dancing on the pool tables" and "adults enjoying their midlife crises"; "cheap drinks" and "killer cheese fries" fuel the "wild" indoor/outdoor scene that some say is "only fun if you barely remember going."

Fat Harry's Bar
| 17 | 12 | 18 | $4 |

4330 St. Charles Ave. (Napoleon Ave.), 504-895-9582

"Another in a long list of prepster undergrad" haunts ("the later it gets, the younger the crowd"), this "college hangout"/sports bar benefits from a "can't-lose" Uptown location "directly on the Mardi Gras parade route" ("if you snag a table outside, never give it up"); expect "cheap pitchers", "reasonable drinks" and "a bit more than the standard bar fare."

528 by Todd English NEW
| _ | _ | _ | VE |

Harrah's Hotel, 228 Poydras St. (Fulton St.), 504-533-6117

Local jazz musicians perform up close on a small stage at this Warehouse District club in a sleekly converted historic space, full of exposed brick and dark-wood beams; newly arrived celebrity chef Todd English runs the show, cooking a light menu of Mediterranean bites and keeping the bar stocked with high-priced Italian wines.

Fritzel's European Jazz Pub   25 16 20 $9
733 Bourbon St. (bet. Orleans & St. Ann Sts.), 504-561-0432
"Escape the Bourbon Street crowd" and "meet some Europeans" at this French Quarter "hole-in-the-wall" known for "traditional" Dixieland jazz; though drinks are pricey and the house "appears ready to fall down", supporters stand up for the "basic" joint that offers "genuine" "local jazz" for "almost no cover."

Funky Pirate   21 14 18 $8
727 Bourbon St. (bet. Orleans & St. Ann Sts.), 504-523-1960; www.tropicalisle.com
Fans of this "no-frills" "Bourbon Street staple" say "all visitors must see Big Al Carson" – and there's a lot of Al to see, since the Quarter's "most foul-mouthed fat man" ("one of the best live acts in town") is 490 pounds of pure Big Easy blues baritone; what most never see coming, however, is the blow delivered by the "deceptively sweet drinks" that taste like "kiddie lemonade."

Gold Mine Saloon   19 13 15 $5
701 Dauphine St. (St. Peter St.), 504-586-0745; www.goldminesaloon.net
The "young and drunk" "shake a tail feather" to "bad Top 40 remixes" "until the sun comes up" at this "cheesy but fun" French Quarter "locals bar"; classic arcade games line the wall, poets read Thursday nights and the "friendly" staff serves "cheap drinks" (like the "signature Flaming Dr. Pepper"); N.B. open Thursday to Saturday only.

Good Friends Bar   18 17 22 $6
740 Dauphine St. (St. Ann St.), 504-566-7191; www.goodfriendsbar.com
"Drink, talk" and "meet boys" at this "quiet conversation bar" in the French Quarter that's "a little more upscale than most of the N'Awlins gay" hangouts; a "nice staff", "gentlemanly" crowd and "friendly" neighborhood vibe that's "comfortable for the non-gay crew too" make up for "measured" cocktails that deliver "only what you pay for."

Handsome Willy's NEW   – – – I
218 S. Robertson St. (Cleveland Ave.), 504-525-0377; www.handsomewillys.com
In an isolated zone of the CBD, this wildly remote haunt now features bullet holes after post-Katrina squatters took a few shots at the walls; with "Ping-Pong, famous hot dogs, live DJs" spinning inside and rock bands jamming on the large patio, it has an underground-party feel.

Hi-ho Lounge
–   –   –   I
2239 St. Claude Ave. (Marigny St.), 504-945-4446
A dive before Katrina, this Marigny club got a clean-up after the flood and now boasts polished wood beams across the high ceiling and shiny retro fixtures that light the room; the drinks served at the art deco bar remain cheap, and it's still a prime spot to catch up-and-coming rockers.

Hookah Café
25   25   16 $10
500 Frenchmen St. (Decatur St.), 504-943-1101;
www.hookah-cafe.com
"Energize before a night of partying" at this "trendy" Faubourg Marigny "harem-style" "loungey bar" where belly dancers and "skillful" DJs create a "unique" atmosphere; though "slow service" roils some ("a shame"), most are willing to wait for the "delicious appetizers", "excellent" drinks and "very enjoyable" hookah smokes.

HOUSE OF BLUES
24   23   19 $12
225 Decatur St. (bet. Bienville Ave. & Iberville St.), 504-529-2583;
www.hob.com
Even if they "say they hate the joint", "everybody goes" to this "worthy" French Quarter link in the live-music chain to see "top-notch talent" and "huge artists" play a "small room" with "wonderful sightlines and great sound"; while some say it suffers from a "corporate clubbing" atmosphere ("love the blues, but this place is all about the greens"), many appreciate the "voodoo theme" and "inspiring" Sunday Gospel Brunch, which "helps you repent Saturday night."

Howlin' Wolf
22   17   18 $9
907 S. Peters St. (Diamond St.), 504-529-5844;
www.thehowlinwolf.com
"Sweat, bump and grind" to the grooves of "diverse" bands both "old and new" at this relocated Warehouse District "musical showplace" that's "one of the real late-night places to see great music"; basically a "big box" of a club that's "not much to look at", the post-Katrina space improves on the old Wolf with "much better sounds" and sightlines.

Igor's Bar & Grill
19   12   18 $6
2133 St. Charles Ave. (Jackson Ave.), 504-568-9811
"Characters abound" at this 24-hour "dive bar" in the Lower Garden District "no-man's-land", where "cheap drinks" (the "best Bloody Mary"), "ginormous" burgers and "energy around the clock" are the draws; the room's not much to look at, but there's "good people-watching on the Avenue."

Jimmy Buffett's Margaritaville Cafe
21   22   20 $10
1104 Decatur St. (Ursuline Ave.), 504-592-2565;
www.margaritavillecafe.com
A possible "surprise visit" by the namesake owner to this French Quarter "Parrothead's paradise" is as much a draw

as the atmosphere, fueled by patrons "singing on stage" with "energetic" live acts; though purists prefer a "real" homegrown haunt to what they label a "mall bar", supporters say it's a "cut above other tourist traps" with a "friendly staff" and "strong if expensive" "boat drinks."

Jin Jean's Lounge NEW　　　– – – M
1700 Louisiana Ave. (Carondelet St.), 504-894-8970
Jazz musicians blow and swing on the half-circle stage surrounded by a low ceiling and glimmering red walls at this new Uptown music club; while the band plays, African-American movers and shakers sip cocktails and nibble on Creole food from the upstairs kitchen, but between sets a DJ spins tunes that get everyone up on the dance floor.

Johnny White's Sports Bar　　22 15 21 $5
720 Bourbon St. (Orleans St.), 504-524-4909
"Get to know the locals" at this "always grungy and always pleasant" "little dive" with "better-than-average Bourbon Street prices" and a staff that's "grateful to have you as a guest"; it's a "legend" that claims to "never, ever close" – even the onslaught of Katrina couldn't stop it from serving "die-hard celebrants."

Kerry Irish Pub　　20 16 21 $6
331 Decatur St. (bet. Bienville Ave. & Conti St.), 504-527-5954; www.kerryirishpub.com
You might "feel like you're in Belfast until you hear a 'ya'll' from the next table" at this Irish pub where "decent prices" and "good service" make patrons "feel at home"; a "great spot for late-afternoon relaxation" or an evening of Gaelic folk tunes, it's "something different" "away from the madness" of the French Quarter.

King Bolden's　　▽ 24 24 21 $7
820 N. Rampart St. (bet. Dumaine & St. Ann Sts.), 504-525-2379
Still "undiscovered", this new "hip spot" radiant with "red mood lighting" and a small "tropical patio" attracts an "eclectic", "local" crowd, including lots of service industry types late at night; it's an "oasis in an otherwise rundown part" of the French Quarter, where DJ Real, a great nephew of the revered jazz player Sidney Bechet, often spins funk, R&B and old-school rap.

Kingpin　　21 18 21 $6
1307 Lyons St. (Prytania St.), 504-891-2373; www.kingpinbar.com
"Everyone seems to know everyone" at this Elvis-adorned Uptown "hipster" joint where the bartenders will "make you smile" and "whip up whatever your heart desires", and "people are always willing to challenge you to a game" on the shuffleboard table (an "unexpected gem"); offbeat bands, spelling bees and crawfish boils, along with carwashes to benefit the city's roller derby team, are often on tap.

Lafitte's Blacksmith Shop
| 25 | 21 | 19 | $6 |

941 Bourbon St. (St. Philip St.), 504-593-9761

"History buffs" and Voodoo Daiquiri tipplers can "get drunk in a national landmark" at this "dark, dank and wonderful" French Quarter "staple" built in 1772; though some say the "rustic", "uncanny" setting has lost "its air of conspiracy", it's still "lit only by candlelight" and filled with the off-key chorus from the "sing-along piano bar" – "miles away" from the madness of Bourbon Street just down the block.

Le Bon Temps Roulé
| 22 | 16 | 19 | $5 |

4801 Magazine St. (Bordeaux St.), 504-895-8117

"Funky doesn't begin to describe" this "quirky", "down and dirty" Uptowner (owned by Corrosion of Conformity's Pepper Keenan), which boasts unbeatable "free live local music" and a "kicking kitchen", serving free oysters to jump-start Friday nights; the "university crowd and baby boomers collide" into a "sweaty mob of people" in the "intimate" concert room; "occasionally celebrities stop in" too.

Le Chat Noir
| 26 | 23 | 23 | $9 |

715 St. Charles Ave. (bet. Girod & Julia Sts.), 504-581-5812;
www.cabaretlechatnoir.com

Comedy, musical and torch-song cabaret buffs "go for the shows" at this sultry, "intimate", "wonderful entertainment" venue in the Warehouse District; with candlelit tables and a black proscenium and piano in the theater, it's "very much a nightclub atmosphere", especially for the "arty over-40 crowd", but cocktail connoisseurs also applaud the "fabulous bartenders" in the separate lobby lounge.

LOA
| 24 | 27 | 23 | $8 |

International House Hotel, 221 Camp St. (Gravier St.),
504-553-9550; www.ihhotel.com

Again voted the city's No. 1 for Decor among New Orleans nightspots, this "phenomenal" CBD lounge enchants reviewers with a "hip and swanky" candlelit interior that plays on a mystical voodoo theme; the chance to "look pretty" and enjoy "intimate conversation" over drinks like the signature Loatini makes believers out of most, though a few are less seduced, claiming it's "trying to be NYC."

Madigans
| 15 | 15 | 17 | $6 |

800 S. Carrollton Ave. (Maple St.), 504-866-9455

"A good happy hour" and decent bar food fit the bill at this "low-key" Carrollton "neighborhood bar" with "cute bartenders"; it's a "favorite for the under-30 crowd", leading dissenters to dismiss it as a "total college hangout."

Maison Bourbon Jazz Club
| 21 | 17 | 17 | $11 |

641 Bourbon St. (bet. St. Peter & Toulouse Sts.), 504-522-8818

"Tap your feet to the beats" of "skilled" "old-time jazz" musicians at this "wonderful" club that helps keep traditional music "alive on Bourbon Street"; the "family-owned establishment" with a beckoning balcony attracts a "nice crowd", though the drinks can be "overpriced."

MAPLE LEAF BAR   27 | 18 | 20 | $5

8316 Oak St. (Cambronne St.), 504-866-9359

"Tuesdays with the Rebirth Brass Band" are "where it's at" for fans of the "fabulously hot, sweaty and energizing" "funk throw-downs" at this "grungy" Carrollton "classic", voted No. 1 for Appeal in New Orleans nightlife; it's a "never boring" "institution for those in need of institutionalization" that makes up for its few faults ("sightlines are bad" and the "sound isn't great") with a "local band of characters", "outrageous and authentic New Orleans musicians" and "dancing on the benches until the sun rises."

Mayfair, The ⊄   23 | 19 | 23 | $7

1505 Amelia St. (St. Charles Ave.), 504-895-9163

"Ring the doorbell" to enter this "funky" Uptown "diamond in the rough" that's a "dive" to some, a "godsend" to others; adorned with "must-see" "Mardi Gras decor", it's "kind of like hanging out in your crazy aunt's rec room", especially when proprietress Gertrude Mayfield, aka Ms. Gertie, is behind the bar.

MID-CITY LANES ROCK 'N' BOWL   27 | 20 | 21 | $7

4133 S. Carrollton Ave. (Tulane Ave.), 504-482-3133;
www.rocknbowl.com

Amid the "cacophony of the tenpins", Mid-City rollers "let down their hair and shake their booties" to "awesome" bands playing everything from blues to zydeco and R&B to rock, at this "one-of-a-kind" bowling alley and dance club; topped off with "greasy late-night food" and "cold brews", it makes "everyone's list for the week" — not necessarily for the '40s-era lanes that will "eat your good ball" but because it might be the "coolest bar in the world."

Milan Lounge   21 | 15 | 24 | $3

1312 Milan St. (Perrier St.), 504-895-1836

"Those in-the-know press the buzzer to gain entrance" to this "teeny" "modern-day speakeasy" Uptown; it "may not be fashionable", but its mix of "cheap drinks", darts that "are taken seriously" and "guaranteed Cubs games on the tube" make it "somehow enticing."

Mimi's in the Marigny   25 | 21 | 21 | $6

2601 Royal St. (Franklin Ave.), 504-872-9868

"Nestled" "out of the way" in the Marigny, this "very chill" "hangout" attracts the 20- to 30-year-old crowd for "dance parties" — like DJ Soul Sister's "not-to-be-missed" Saturday shows — in the upstairs room with its balcony and "funky, falling-apart couches" or to the more "romantic" downstairs space with a pool table; "magnificent" bartenders and "delicious" tapas add to the draw.

Molly's at the Market   24 | 21 | 24 | $6
1107 Decatur St. (Ursuline Ave.), 504-525-5169;
www.mollysatthemarket.net
Expect "street punks, lawyers" and "everything in-between"
at this "low-key" "real Irish bar", a French Quarter "institution" that "stayed open straight through Katrina"; loyal-
ists agree the "great Bloody Marys", frozen Irish coffee
and "the best jukebox in New Orleans" further the appeal
of "the kind of place every town should have, but few do."

Monkey Hill Bar   21 | 22 | 20 | $7
6100 Magazine St. (Webster St.), 504-899-4800
"Pretty people and preppies" populate this "upscale"
"Uptown oasis" where a "lively" vibe, "great jukebox" and
flattering "low lighting" create a "good-for-singles"
scene; though a few find it "a bit stiff" ("like drinking in a
Talbot's"), an "amazing wine list", "comfy sofas" and
"beautiful bartenders" pouring "excellent drinks" have
helped it "quickly climb the favorites list of many locals."

Ms. Mae's The Club ⊭   19 | 10 | 19 | $3
4336 Magazine St. (Napoleon Ave.), 504-895-9401
"If you're low on cash" head to this "drunkards nirvana"
Uptown, named the *Survey*'s Best Bang for the Buck among
bars, where "frat boys, hipsters", "crusty" boozers and pro-
fessors "get loaded" on as "strong-as-you-can-imagine"
$1 drinks 24/7; sure, it can be a "depressing" "dive", but
regulars swear "you'll always leave this place with a story."

Old Absinthe House   23 | 20 | 20 | $9
240 Bourbon St. (Bienville St.), 504-523-3181;
www.oldabsinthehouse.com
"Young and old professionals" and tourists add their calling
cards to the wall at this "atmospheric" "landmark", which
fans call the "only decent joint left on Bourbon Street"; the
"potent" signature Absinthe House Frappe helps explain the
"friendly, intoxicated crowd", even if more sober assessors
question the allure of "just another" "neighborhood bar."

Old Point Bar   19 | 16 | 20 | $6
545 Patterson Dr. (Oliver St.), Algiers, 504-364-0950;
www.oldpointbar.com
"Relaxed and neighborly", this "funky", "unique" Algiers
Point "local hangout" next to the ferry landing also "attracts a non-neighborhood crowd"; "you can always count
on it for great live music" and "fun late-night jamming"
sounds that "spill out onto the street."

One Eyed Jacks   24 | 23 | 19 | $9
615 Toulouse St. (Chartres St.), 504-569-8361;
www.oneeyedjacks.net
This French Quarter "indie central", which "just plain
looks cool" with "bordello decor" ("velvet on the walls",

etc.), books "great" local and national acts that attract a "diverse" crowd of "gay, straight, black, white, hipster, rapper and geek"; though a few feel it's "too hip for its own good" and the drinks are "kinda pricey", most agree its "mesmerizing go-go dancers" of both sexes during the "awesome '80s night" make for "a good time."

Oz ⊄
| 21 | 20 | 21 | $6 |

800 Bourbon St. (St. Ann St.), 504-593-9491;
www.oznewrleans.com
You'll know "you're not in Kansas anymore" at this "scorchingly gay", "energy-filled" club with the "hunkiest go-go boys in the French Quarter"; the "wildly varying" cover "can be high", but most willingly pay to join the "youngish" (some say "barely-out-of-diapers") crowd on the dance floor or the balconies overlooking Bourbon Street; N.B. it's open 24 hours on Friday and Saturday.

PAT O'BRIEN'S
| 26 | 23 | 20 | $10 |

718 St. Peter St. (Royal St.), 504-525-4823; www.patobriens.com
"Two Hurricanes and you'll hit the floor" at the "famous" (and "apropos") drink's French Quarter originator, a "lively" "legend in the Big Easy" voted the city's Most Popular nightspot; "locals don't mind mingling with the tourists" as part of the "wild ride", and though some grouse it's "pricey" ("don't forget to return those glasses for your deposit"), most speak fondly of the "flaming fountain" in the "lovely courtyard" and the "ridiculously entertaining" dueling pianos.

Phoenix, The ⊄
| ∇ 19 | 9 | 24 | $5 |

941 Elysian Fields Ave. (bet. Burgundy & N. Rampart Sts.),
504-945-9264
"Don't bring your mama" to this "truly wild" gay leather bar in the Faubourg Marigny that carries the torch of "New York or San Francisco in the '70s"; a "dirty place to have fun", it's "not for the weak of heart", but "those who dare" will find "frisky patrons", "friendly bartenders" and "strong and cheap drinks."

Polo Lounge
| ∇ 28 | 27 | 26 | $10 |

Windsor Court Hotel, 300 Gravier St. (S. Peter St.), 504-523-6000;
www.windsorcourthotel.com
At this "swanky place for high-society hanky panky" inside the Windsor Court Hotel, guests find an "elegant", "intimate" spot to "enjoy a good scotch" or a champagne-topped Polo Martini while a piano player performs jazz standards; as one swell says, "it's always a safe retreat."

PRESERVATION HALL ⊄
| 26 | 17 | 16 | $9 |

726 St. Peter St. (bet. Bourbon & Royal Sts.), 504-523-8939;
www.preservationhall.com
Guests "step back about 80 years" and "worship at the feet of the masters" playing the "fantastic rhythms of

Dixieland" at this French Quarter "church of jazz"; given the fading facade, "creaky floors" and hard wooden benches, some call it "a museum posing as a nightclub", and indeed, it offers "no drinks, no food, no space" – just a "live jam hall" where it's "all about the music."

RAWHIDE 2010 ⊘ | 21 | 13 | 24 | $4 |

740 Burgundy St. (St. Ann St.), 504-525-8106;
www.rawhide2010.com
"Bears", "cowboys and leather queens abound" at this Vieux Carré "jewel" of a "cruise bar" whose "friendly bartenders" slinging "strong drinks" earn it top ratings for Service among nightspots; it's definitely on the "wild side of the Quarter" and "not for the timid", with plenty of "dark corners" for "interactions with other convivial patrons."

Razzoo Bar & Patio | 18 | 15 | 16 | $6 |

511 Bourbon St. (bet. St. Louis & Toulouse Sts.), 504-522-5100
"Dance with people you don't even know" at this "rowdy (and sometimes raunchy)" French Quarter "late-night" "hangout" staffed with "scantily clad waitresses" delivering "quality drinks for the money"; some swear it's a "drunken tourist bar" full of "lecherous conventiongoers and frat boys" – which is probably why it's "easy to hook up here."

R Bar | 21 | 19 | 18 | $6 |

Royal Street Inn, 1431 Royal St. (Esplanade Ave.), 504-948-7499;
www.royalstreetinn.com
This "space-punk rocket ship of a bar" – decked out with old airline seats and skeletons on choppers overhead – is a "funky, local" "well-liked neighborhood spot" "off the beaten path" in the Marigny; "late at night" "everyone gets a little raucous" while sipping "reasonably priced drinks" and watching muted "cult classic movies", or on Mondays taking a seat in the barber chair for a $10 haircut with a free shot.

Red Eye Bar & Grill | 19 | 14 | 19 | $7 |

852 S. Peters St. (bet. Julia & St. Joseph Sts.), 504-593-9393
1057 Veterans Memorial Blvd. (Sena Dr.), Metairie, 504-833-6900
www.redeyegrill.net
"Eccentric locals" "stumble and mumble" at these Warehouse District and Metairie "low-key beer halls"; they're "nothing fancy", with only the "minimal atmosphere" of exposed rafters and ceiling fans, but the late-night drinks, food and "'80s music" make it a stop for some.

Republic New Orleans NEW | 22 | 22 | 20 | $8 |

828 S. Peters St. (bet. Julia & St. Joseph Sts.), 504-528-8282;
www.republicnola.com
Fans flock to this "wonderful" Warehouse District club known for "crowded" dance nights and a "great variety" of live acts, "applauding its attempt to bring some class to the city's nightlife" with a dress code and a limited-access

policy – you "have to be on a guest list" to get upstairs, though some say "residents make fun of V.I.P. sections"; still, all agree about the "available, accommodating" staff and "great decor."

Rivershack Tavern　　　　　| 23 | 21 | 20 | $5 |
3449 River Rd. (Shrewsbury Rd.), Jefferson, 504-834-4938
"Out of the tourist orbit" in Jefferson Parish, this "old-school" riverside roadhouse (or should we say, levee-house) still has its "tacky ashtray" collection, "funky" mannequin-legged barstools and "authentic grubby, not fake grubby" atmosphere, even after a post-Katrina redo; folks "dressed up or down" gather for live music, burgers and a "few too many", including microbrews and a "can't-be-beat" "root beer on draft."

Saturn Bar ⌿　　　　▽ | 24 | 20 | 23 | $6 |
3067 St. Claude Ave. (Clouet St.), 504-949-7532
"Like drinking in Fred Sanford's yard" with junk piled everywhere, this "eclectic" Bywater dive and "national treasure" in a "sketchy neighborhood" has "walls adorned with great neon and wild artwork"; the "one-of-a-kind owner", O'Neil Broyard, died shortly after Katrina, but his nephew "is keeping the dive alive" with some improvements – no more cat stink – and some losses – a modern Internet jukebox replaces the classic machine soaked by the flood.

Snake & Jake's　　　　　| 19 | 13 | 18 | $4 |
Christmas Club Lounge
7612 Oak St. (Hillary St.), 504-861-2802
"If you can find the place, you're probably too sober to be here" razz regulars of this "dark and dirty" "dump" Uptown, which "succeeds in being seedy" with couches to be "avoided at all costs" and a host of "shady characters" who don't pour in till around 3 AM; the bar "takes great pride in selling Schlitz" and mixing "terrific Bloody Marys", but don't let its low-key offerings hold you back, since rumor has it "if you get naked, you drink for free."

Snug Harbor Jazz Bistro　　| 26 | 18 | 20 | $9 |
626 Frenchmen St. (Chartres St.), 504-949-0696;
www.snugjazz.com
"Where the famous acts perform on Frenchmen Street", this "cozy" jazz venue draws "serious fans" to catch "some of the finest musicians in the world" along with "top-quality" local talents like Charmaine Neville and Ellis Marsalis; its "intimate" space with "cocktail seating" sets the stage for performances, while "good food" is served in the adjoining dining room.

Spotted Cat ⌿　　　　　| 23 | 16 | 18 | $6 |
623 Frenchmen St. (Chartres St.), 504-943-3887
Swinging tunes "transport the listener to another era" at this "tiny", "crowded and delightful" Marigny spot that's

most renowned for its "hot club" sets by the New Orleans Jazz Vipers; though it's often a squeeze, once you're past the door and "only 10 feet away" from the stage, you might purr there's "no more relaxed and jazzier place on the planet."

St. Joe's Bar   24 23 20 $5
5535 Magazine St. (Octavia St.), 504-899-3744
"Adorned with crosses" and icons in "honor of its saintly name", this "laid-back" Uptowner fills up with a "youngish crowd" of "yuppies and Tulane students" shooting pool in the "hallwaylike" "dark room" and drinking "badass" blueberry mojitos; the back patio heightens the mood with "romantic red paper lanterns" illuminating an "amazing Asian garden."

Swizzle Stick Bar   24 26 24 $10
Loews New Orleans Hotel, 300 Poydras St. (S. Peters St.), 504-595-3305; www.cafeadelaide.com
"Chic" touches set the mood at this "comfortable", "beautiful" cocktail spot inside Café Adelaide, a young "Brennan family offshoot" in the CBD's Loews Hotel; manning a "snazzy" horseshoe bar built around a block of ice, mixologists craft an array of "innovative" drinks, including a happy hour special every day.

TIPITINA'S   27 21 19 $8
501 Napoleon Ave. (Tchoupitoulas St.), 504-895-8477; www.tipitinas.com
"Dance till your feet bleed" to the tunes of "top-notch talent" playing funk, soul and rock at this Uptown "American classic" with a "small-town feel"; the "weathered" but "nice-sized" space gets so "mightily crowded" at night that the "walls sweat", but the "famous" Cajun fais do-do parties on Sunday afternoons offer a little extra stepping room for "fabulous, friendly dancers."

Tommy's Wine Bar NEW   - - - E
752 Tchoupitoulas St. (Notre Dame St.), 504-525-4790
With its large dark room lit by gaslights and full of private nooks, this swanky new Warehouse District wine bar adds a touch of romantic sophistication to the neighborhood; a pianist plays nightly, and the bartenders at the elaborate hand-carved bar pour reds, whites and bubblies from the cellar's 120 vintages, as well as rare selections of whiskey, scotch and cognac.

Tropical Isle   20 14 19 $7
600 Bourbon St. (Toulouse St.), 504-529-1728
721 Bourbon St. (Orleans St.), 504-529-4109
www.tropicalisle.com
Tourists, college kids and "lots of bachelor and bachelorette parties" join in the booze-fueled bacchanal at this French Quarter twosome, "home of the Hand Grenade" (a "toxic" cocktail in a neon-green cup – "don't be lulled into

thinking it's fruit punch") and other "crazy drinks in crazy glasses"; though they both boast the same "cheap luau-like decor", the 721 address is big for "throwing beads off the balcony."

VAUGHAN'S LOUNGE   26 | 20 | 23 | $5
800 Lesseps St. (Dauphine St.), 504-947-5562
"People drive from all over" to this "sagging, tin-roofed" "neighborhood bar" in Bywater to catch the "sublime" jazz trumpeter Kermit Ruffins and his Barbecue Swingers, whose "legendary", "magic" Thursday night shows "usher in a festive weekend"; always bubbly with "cold longnecks" and a "truly eclectic crowd" that spills out-side, it "oozes old-school charm."

Whiskey Blue   23 | 24 | 20 | $11
*W New Orleans, 333 Poydras St. (bet. S. Peters &
Tchoupitoulas Sts.), 504-525-9444; www.mocbars.com*
"New York meets New Orleans" at this "ultratrendy" "candlelit" W hotel lounge in the CBD, which is "like step-ping into a *Sex and the City* episode", with its "slick" atmo-sphere, "comfy couches and a plush bed" for cushioning plenty of "young" "beautiful people"; DJs sometimes spin tunes and the "drinks are terrific" but "pricey", so it's "bet-ter if someone else is paying."

Nightlife Indexes

LOCATIONS

Bywater
Saturn Bar
Vaughan's Lounge

Carrollton
Carrollton Station
Cooter Brown's
Madigans
Maple Leaf

CBD (Central Business District)
Handsome Willy's
Loa
Polo Lounge
Swizzle Stick
Whiskey Blue

Faubourg Marigny
Applebarrel
Café Brasil
d.b.a.
Dragon's Den
Hi-ho Lounge
Hookah Café
Mimi's in Marigny
Phoenix, The
R Bar
Snug Harbor Jazz
Spotted Cat

French Quarter
Abbey, The
Bombay Club
Bourbon Pub/Parade
Bourbon St. Blues
Cafe Lafitte in Exile
Cajun Cabin
Carousel Bar
Cat's Meow
Checkpoint Charlie's
Corner Pocket
Coyote Ugly
Donna's B&G
Dungeon, The
Famous Door
Fritzel's Jazz
Funky Pirate

Gold Mine Saloon
Good Friends Bar
House of Blues
Jimmy Buffett's
Johnny White's
Kerry Irish Pub
King Bolden's
Lafitte's Blacksmith
Maison Jazz
Molly's at Market
Old Absinthe Hse.
One Eyed Jacks
Oz
Pat O'Brien's
Preservation Hall
Rawhide 2010
Razzoo Bar & Patio
Tropical Isle

Garden District
Columns Hotel

Garden District (Lower)
Avenue Pub
Big Top Gallery
Bridge Lounge
Igor's B&G

Jefferson
Rivershack Tavern

Metairie
Red Eye B&G

Mid-City
Banks Street B&G
Bulldog, The
Chickie Wah Wah
Mid-City Lanes

Uptown
Balcony Bar
Boot, The
Bruno's
Bulldog, The
Dos Jefes Cigar
F&M Patio Bar
Fat Harry's

Jin Jean's Lounge
Kingpin
Le Bon Temps Roulé
Mayfair, The
Milan Lounge
Monkey Hill
Ms. Mae's
Snake & Jake's
St. Joe's Bar
Tipitina's

Warehouse District
Circle Bar
528 by Todd English
Howlin' Wolf
Le Chat Noir
Red Eye B&G
Republic
Tommy's Wine Bar

West Bank
Old Point Bar

SPECIAL APPEALS

(Indexes list the best in each category. Multi-location nightspots' features may vary by branch. For some categories, schedules may vary; call ahead to check.)

After Hours
Checkpoint Charlie's
Chickie Wah Wah
F&M Patio Bar
Hi-ho Lounge
Howlin' Wolf
Lafitte's Blacksmith
Le Bon Temps Roulé
Molly's at Market
Oz
R Bar

After Work
Bridge Lounge
Bulldog, The
Columns Hotel
Dos Jefes Cigar
Fat Harry's
Kingpin
Loa
Molly's at Market
Monkey Hill
Polo Lounge

Cocktail Experts
Bridge Lounge
Carousel Bar
Columns Hotel
Loa
Polo Lounge
St. Joe's Bar
Swizzle Stick

Dance Clubs
Bourbon Pub/Parade
Dungeon, The
One Eyed Jacks
Oz
Republic

Dancing
Banks Street B&G
Bombay Club
Boot, The
Bourbon Pub/Parade
Bourbon St. Blues
Café Brasil
Cafe Lafitte in Exile
Cajun Cabin
Cat's Meow
King Bolden's
Maple Leaf
Mid-City Lanes
One Eyed Jacks
Oz
Razzoo Bar & Patio
Republic
Tipitina's
Vaughan's Lounge

Dives
Abbey, The
Avenue Pub
Checkpoint Charlie's
Circle Bar
Gold Mine Saloon
Igor's B&G
Johnny White's
Le Bon Temps Roulé
Maple Leaf
Mayfair, The
Milan Lounge
Molly's at Market
Ms. Mae's
Saturn Bar
Snake & Jake's
Vaughan's Lounge

DJs
Bourbon Pub/Parade
Dungeon, The
Handsome Willy's
Hookah Café
Mimi's in Marigny
One Eyed Jacks
Oz

Republic
Whiskey Blue

Fine Food Too
Bombay Club
Bridge Lounge
Jin Jean's Lounge
Mimi's in Marigny
Snug Harbor Jazz
Swizzle Stick

Gay/Lesbian
Bourbon Pub/Parade
Cafe Lafitte in Exile
Corner Pocket
Good Friends Bar
Oz
Phoenix, The
Rawhide 2010

Happy Hour
Avenue Pub
Balcony Bar
Bridge Lounge
Bruno's
Bulldog, The
Circle Bar
Columns Hotel
Cooter Brown's
d.b.a.
Kingpin
Mimi's in Marigny
Monkey Hill
St. Joe's Bar
Swizzle Stick

Hotel Bars
Columns Hotel
   Columns Hotel
Harrah's Hotel
   528 by Todd English
Hotel Monteleone
   Carousel Bar
International House Hotel
   Loa
Loews New Orleans Hotel
   Swizzle Stick
Windsor Court Hotel
   Polo Lounge
W New Orleans
   Whiskey Blue

Jazz Clubs
Donna's B&G
Fritzel's Jazz
Maison Jazz
Preservation Hall
Snug Harbor Jazz
Spotted Cat
Vaughan's Lounge

Jukeboxes
Applebarrel
Avenue Pub
Balcony Bar
Bruno's
Checkpoint Charlie's
Circle Bar
Cooter Brown's
Coyote Ugly
Donna's B&G
Dungeon, The
F&M Patio Bar
Fat Harry's
Funky Pirate
Kingpin
Lafitte's Blacksmith
Le Bon Temps Roulé
Maple Leaf
Mayfair, The
Mid-City Lanes
Molly's at Market
Ms. Mae's
Old Absinthe Hse.
Pat O'Brien's
Rawhide 2010
St. Joe's Bar
Tropical Isle

Live Music
Abbey, The
Bombay Club
Café Brasil
Cajun Cabin
Carousel Bar
Carrollton Station
Checkpoint Charlie's
Circle Bar
Columns Hotel
d.b.a.
Dos Jefes Cigar

Dungeon, The
Good Friends Bar
Hi-ho Lounge
Jimmy Buffett's
Kerry Irish Pub
King Bolden's
Kingpin
Lafitte's Blacksmith
Le Bon Temps Roulé
Le Chat Noir
Mimi's in Marigny
Old Point Bar
Pat O'Brien's
Polo Lounge
Razzoo Bar & Patio
Rivershack Tavern
Swizzle Stick
Tommy's Wine Bar
Tropical Isle

Local Favorites

Applebarrel
Banks Street B&G
Bridge Lounge
Bulldog, The
Café Brasil
Carousel Bar
Circle Bar
Columns Hotel
Cooter Brown's
d.b.a.
Donna's B&G
Dos Jefes Cigar
F&M Patio Bar
Howlin' Wolf
Igor's B&G
Kingpin
Le Bon Temps Roulé
Maple Leaf
Mid-City Lanes
Mimi's in Marigny
Molly's at Market
Saturn Bar
Snake & Jake's
Snug Harbor Jazz
Spotted Cat
St. Joe's Bar
Tipitina's
Vaughan's Lounge

Music Clubs

(See also Jazz Clubs)
Applebarrel
Chickie Wah Wah
Dragon's Den
House of Blues
Howlin' Wolf
Jin Jean's Lounge
Maple Leaf
Mid-City Lanes
One Eyed Jacks
Republic
Tipitina's

Noteworthy Newcomers

Chickie Wah Wah
528 by Todd English
Handsome Willy's
Jin Jean's Lounge
Republic
Tommy's Wine Bar

Old New Orleans

(50+ yrs.; Year opened;
* building)
1722 Lafitte's Blacksmith*
1750 Preservation Hall*
1800 Molly's at Market*
1811 Cat's Meow*
1815 Old Absinthe Hse.
1831 Fritzel's Jazz*
1835 Dungeon, The*
1883 Columns Hotel*
1923 Pat O'Brien's
1933 Cafe Lafitte in Exile
1934 Abbey, The
1934 Bruno's
1949 Carousel Bar

Outdoor Spaces

Garden
Bombay Club
Patio/Terrace
Balcony Bar
Bourbon Pub/Parade
Bruno's
Bulldog, The
Cafe Lafitte in Exile
Carrollton Station
Cat's Meow

Chickie Wah Wah
Circle Bar
Columns Hotel
Dos Jefes Cigar
F&M Patio Bar
Funky Pirate
Good Friends Bar
Handsome Willy's
House of Blues
Jimmy Buffett's
King Bolden's
Lafitte's Blacksmith
Le Bon Temps Roulé
Madigans
Maple Leaf
Old Absinthe Hse.
Pat O'Brien's
Phoenix, The
Razzoo Bar & Patio
Rivershack Tavern
St. Joe's Bar
Tropical Isle

Sidewalk
Boot, The
Bridge Lounge
Bulldog, The
Cooter Brown's
Fat Harry's
Igor's B&G
Vaughan's Lounge

People-Watching
Bourbon Pub/Parade
Café Brasil
Circle Bar
Columns Hotel
Hookah Café
Loa
Maple Leaf
Molly's at Market
Polo Lounge
Whiskey Blue

Pool Tables
Avenue Pub
Balcony Bar
Banks Street B&G

Boot, The
Bruno's
Cafe Lafitte in Exile
Carrollton Station
Checkpoint Charlie's
Chickie Wah Wah
Cooter Brown's
Dos Jefes Cigar
Dungeon, The
F&M Patio Bar
Fat Harry's
Gold Mine Saloon
Good Friends Bar
Hi-ho Lounge
Howlin' Wolf
Igor's B&G
Kerry Irish Pub
Le Bon Temps Roulé
Madigans
Mayfair, The
Mimi's in Marigny
Monkey Hill
Ms. Mae's
Phoenix, The
Rawhide 2010
R Bar
Rivershack Tavern
Saturn Bar
St. Joe's Bar
Tropical Isle

Romantic
Bombay Club
Carousel Bar
Columns Hotel
Lafitte's Blacksmith
Loa
Polo Lounge
Snug Harbor Jazz

Sports Bars
Boot, The
Bruno's
Bulldog, The
Cooter Brown's
Johnny White's

Attractions

*While most historical sites and museums survived Katrina intact and are listed below, much of New Orleans was devastated. Visitors can take one of several guided bus tours, to view these areas in a responsible, educational way and learn about possibilities for reconstruction. A few options are **Cajun Encounters** (www.cajunencounters.com), **Gray Line** (www.grayline.com) and **Tours by Isabelle** (www.toursbyisabelle.com).*

Most Popular

1. Audubon Aquarium
2. French Market
3. Audubon Zoo
4. Nat'l World War II Museum
5. Audubon Park

Top Appeal

29 Nat'l World War II Museum
28 Audubon Zoo
27 Audubon Aquarium
   Jackson Square
   Audubon Park

| A | F | S | $ |

Ashé Cultural Arts Center

| – | – | – | I |

1712 Oretha Castle Haley Blvd. (Euterpe St.), 504-569-9070; www.ashecac.org
Established and emerging African-American painters, performers and writers gather in this community-oriented, multiuse Central City facility that brings together art exhibits and plays with drumming circles and dance classes in a sleek, lofty 6,600-sq.-ft. space.

AUDUBON AQUARIUM OF THE AMERICAS

| 27 | 26 | 24 | M |

1 Canal St. (Convention Center Blvd.), 504-581-4629; 800-774-7394; www.auduboninstitute.org
Surveyors rate this "wonderful", "exotic" aquarium on the Mississippi River edge of the French Quarter the city's

Most Popular attraction for its "world-class exhibits" that some say are "second only to Monterey, CA"; "fantastic fins", "entertaining eels", "amazing" white alligators and a "caring staff" make a visit to this "gorgeous" "gem" "a blast for everyone, kids and grown-ups alike."

Audubon Park   27 | 21 | 16 | $0

6500 St. Charles Ave. (bet. Calhoun & Walnut Sts.), 504-581-4629; 800-774-7394; www.auduboninstitute.org

"Dripping with Spanish moss and Southern charm", "ancient" oaks "still standing after Katrina" create a "green oasis" in this "jewel of Uptown New Orleans" with its "well-kept" "bike and walking paths" and "fabulous golf course"; "adjacent to the zoo", it's a "serene", "wonderful" place to "feed the ducks", "ride bikes" or just "waste away a day" "with a good book."

AUDUBON ZOO   28 | 26 | 23 | M

6500 Magazine St. (Exposition Blvd.), 504-861-2537; 866-487-2966; www.auduboninstitute.org

"Da monkeys, dey all aks fo' you" at this "outstanding" zoo, a "modern marvel" Uptown that's deemed a "great family attraction" with a "dedicated staff" and "user-friendly layout"; for the ultimate New Orleans experience, "cruise on the steamboat" there and catch some "local flavor" at the "not-to-be-missed" swamp exhibit that's "so authentic they post nutria recipes."

Beauregard-Keyes House   21 | 22 | 20 | I

1113 Chartres St. (Ursuline St.), 504-523-7257

A visit to this little known, "nicely restored" Vieux Carré mansion is "a must for fans of [author] Francis Parkinson-Keyes" and appealing to "history buffs"; aside from an "extensive doll collection" it's "not riveting for kids", but "informative" docents provide an "interesting glimpse" into ante- and postbellum French Quarter life.

Cabildo   23 | 23 | 20 | I

701 Chartres St. (St. Peter St.), 504-568-6968; 800-568-6968; lsm.crt.state.la.us

"Fascinating" any time of year but a particularly "cool respite" when it's hot, this "exquisite" 1790s Spanish-style building on Jackson Square is the flagship of the Louisiana State Museum complex; Napoleon's death mask is one "highlight", but "you can spend a day" learning what New Orleans was like "before the Hurricane – the drink, not the natural disaster – hit Bourbon Street."

Contemporary Arts Center   22 | 24 | 21 | I

900 Camp St. (bet. Andrew Higgins Dr. & St. Joseph St.), 504-528-3805; www.cacno.org

This "ultracool" Warehouse District space is a "hip", "vibrant" "showcase" for "great" "local artwork" and "interesting" traveling shows that "push the envelope in the best way"; though critics contend "it doesn't compare with New York City or Chicago" galleries, CAC fans "highly recommend" it for its "eclectic collection" of "plays, music, exhibits" and "performance art" offered year-round.

FRENCH MARKET   23 | 17 | 18 | $0 |

Decatur St. (bet. Esplanade Ave. & Jackson Sq.), 504-522-2621; www.frenchmarket.org

"Kitschy yet cool", this French Quarter "shopper's paradise" makes a "great stroll full of history" with an "eclectic gumbo" of "wonderful spices", T-shirts, "irresistible mementos" and "beads, beads, beads"; though the "charmingly displayed junk" can be "hit-or-miss", fans come to "wander, people-watch" and "haggle with vendors" for a "unique experience" that's "touristy, but in a good way."

Gallier House   ∇ 26 | 24 | 23 | I |

1118-32 Royal St. (bet. Governor Nicholls & Ursuline Sts.), 504-525-5661; www.hgghh.org

The former home of one of Victorian New Orleans' "premier architects", this "exquisitely detailed and maintained" French Quarter house museum boasts "several innovative" (for the time) features such as running water, skylights and copper bathtubs; "informative guides", seasonal decorative "dressings" reminiscent of "the old times" and a "great gift shop" make it "fun for the entire family."

Hermann-Grima House   26 | 26 | 24 | I |

820 St. Louis St. (Bourbon St.), 504-525-5661; www.hgghh.org

This "very well-preserved" and faithfully restored mid-19th-century French Quarter mansion, complete with a courtyard and stable, offers a close "look into the lifestyles" of the era's rich and famous Creole families, as well as edification for those "interested in the history of architecture"; the "great docents" lead lively tours, and the particularly memorable cooking demonstrations at the outdoor "pre–Civil War working kitchen" "make you realize how different things used to be."

Historic New Orleans Collections   25 | 25 | 24 | I |

533 Royal St. (bet. St. Louis & Toulouse Sts.), 504-523-4662; www.hnoc.org

"A diamond in the midst of the Quarter", this "enlightening" museum holds an "amazing collection of artifacts and books, papers and plans" that are "painstakingly kept by professionals who care"; its multiple buildings encompass the Williams Gallery, Research Center and Residence (a former "not-so-humble abode"), which all provide a fascinating, "immense" "archive of New Orleans" along with "interesting special events."

Houmas House Plantation
| | | | – | – | – | M |

40136 Hwy. 942, Darrow, 225-473-9380; www.houmashouse.com
Once the largest plantation in America, this rarefied
River Road estate sold sugar at a clip until the great
flood of 1927 and the ensuing Depression, and was restored in 2003 when new owners decorated the Greek
Revival mansion with period antiques and enlivened its
surrounding 12-acre site with elaborate gardens; leisurely
afternoon tours often lead to dinner on the grounds at
Latil's Landing Restaurant.

Jackson Square
| 27 | 18 | 15 | $0 |

Chartres to St. Ann Sts., Decatur to St. Peter Sts.;
www.jackson-square.com
"Hundreds of years of history" unfold throughout this "pic-
turesque" park and strong contender for the "heart of the
city", named for hometown hero Andrew Jackson (de-
picted in the central equestrian sculpture) and bordered
by the Mississippi River and St. Louis Cathedral; in addition
to its "amazing architecture" and some of the "best street
theater" in town ("the starving artists, fortune tellers, performers are sprinkling back"), it makes a "lovely place for
people-watching" to the rhythm of "horses pulling car-
riages" and "sweet jazz played on the corner."

Jean Lafitte National
Historical Park
| 26 | 20 | 19 | $0 |

6588 Barataria Blvd., Marrero, 504-589-2330 Ext. 10;
www.nps.gov/Jela
Named for one of the most colorful Barataria pirates of old,
this "swamp setting" with its "lush marshland" "just outside the city" is a "gem" of greater New Orleans; both locals and tourists tout it as a "terrific place to see some
gators and enjoy the bayou" while taking "wonderful walking paths" and guided canoe tours with "informed
rangers" – and it's "especially gorgeous" in the spring
"when the irises are in bloom."

Lafayette Cemetery No. 1
| ▽ 25 | 14 | 12 | I |

1400 Washington Ave. (Prytania St.), 888-721-7493;
www.saveourcemeteries.org
Amid the mansions of the Garden District lies a "whole different world" "unlike anything you've ever seen" – this
19th-century site of "beautiful" above-ground tombs,
which reflect the "weight of history and lives past"; it
makes a smart stop for a tour before lunch at Commander's
Palace (right across the street), since it closes at 2:30 PM
weekdays and noon on Saturday (closed Sunday).

Longue Vue House and Gardens
| 26 | 25 | 24 | I |

7 Bamboo Rd. (Metairie Rd.), 504-488-5488; www.longuevue.com
The "absolutely beautiful, extremely well-kept" and
flower-filled gardens designed by Ellen Biddle Shipman

are the buzz of this Old Metairie national landmark – an "incredible city estate" built in 1942 for Edgar Bloom Stern, a cotton broker, and his wife, Edith Rosenwald Stern, a Sears-Roebuck heiress; "renewed and regrowing" post-Katrina, it remains a "wonderful hidden treasure" enhanced by the "great children's discovery area", gift shop "without equal" and events that enchant "in the spring" and "around the holidays."

Louisiana Children's Museum _ | _ | _ | I
420 Julia St. (bet. Magazine & Tchoupitoulas Sts.), 504-523-1357; www.lcm.org
Families flock to this most playful of places for a variety of hands-on hijinks – like piloting a tugboat down the Mississippi or anchoring the evening news – and even the littlest of visitors have a special nook for climbing and hiding; special art programs and exhibitions round out the experience at this Warehouse District establishment, as does the well-stocked museum shop.

Memorial Hall/ Confederate Museum 20 | 16 | 16 | I
929 Camp St. (bet. Andrew Higgins Dr. & St. Joseph St.), 504-523-4522; www.confederatemuseum.com
Founded by Confederate veterans, this "strange", "forlorn"-looking Warehouse District museum is "controversial" for sure, but history buffs say it "deserves to be better known" for its "huge, varied collection of Civil War memorabilia"; many find it an "interesting" "balance to the World War II Museum" nearby, even if it's "not worth a stop by itself."

NATIONAL WORLD WAR II MUSEUM 29 | 29 | 26 | M
(fka National D-Day Museum)
945 Magazine St. (Andrew Higgins Dr.), 504-527-6012; www.nationalww2museum.org
"Moving, inspiring and humbling", this "world-class" Warehouse District "must-see" (founded by historian Stephen Ambrose as the National D-Day Museum) presents an "outstanding" collection that spans "everything from rationing to V-Day", "diary entries to uniforms", and "doesn't pull any punches" in conveying the "terror and trauma of war"; rated No. 1 for Appeal among Attractions, it features exhibits covering "both the European and Pacific theaters" and engaging docents ("a highlight") who "fascinate even the non–history buff", leaving visitors with a "great appreciation for the men and women who served."

New Orleans Botanical Garden 26 | 24 | 21 | I
City Park, Victory Ave. (off Roosevelt Mall Dr.), 504-483-9386; www.neworleanscitypark.com
"Still rebounding" from the hurricane, this WPA-era City Park garden, which suffered massive wind damage and

flooding, has been replanted to become a "post-Katrina oasis of beauty" that's "soothing to the soul"; its "great array" of "native plants", notably its forest of "ancient" live oaks (the largest in the world), is complemented by Enrique Alferez's sculptures, a miniature train garden that operates on the weekends and seasonal traditions like "music in the summer and pretty lights during the holidays."

New Orleans City Park   23 | 16 | 15 | $0 |
1 Palm Dr. (Marconi Dr.), 504-482-4888;
www.neworleanscitypark.com
It was "hit tremendously hard by Katrina" and "a lot of work" still needs to be done, but this 1,500-acre Mid-City "treasure", one of the largest parks in the country, is "slowly being restored" by "scores of volunteers"; home to the New Orleans Museum of Art, the Sydney and Walda Besthoff Sculpture Garden, Botanical Garden and Storyland amusement park (crafted by Mardi Gras float designers), it's "still a great place to walk, jog or bike" and to visit during December's light-festooned Celebration in the Oaks.

New Orleans Museum of Art   26 | 26 | 23 | I |
(aka NOMA)
City Park, 1 Collins Diboll Circle (Esplanade Ave.), 504-488-2631;
www.noma.org
"One of the city's greatest assets", this "beautiful beaux arts building" and its "very fine collection" fortunately remain "intact" despite Katrina's impact on surrounding City Park; its "awesome glass display", "extensive" European and American paintings and pre-Columbian pieces "will keep you riveted for hours", but be sure to leave time for the "spectacular" sculpture garden, perhaps "the number one way to introduce young people to art while giving them room to run around."

Oak Alley Plantation   – | – | – | M |
3645 Hwy. 18 (Oak Alley Farm Rd.), Vacherie, 225-265-2151;
www.oakalleyplantation.com
Countryside trekkers have a soft spot for this "incredible antebellum plantation", which offers a "great tour" of its "magnificent" oak allée and grand Southern mansion ("where *Interview with the Vampire* was filmed"); you can rent a car and plan for a "full-day of activity" on 'Plantation Road' (River Road) – "just be sure you have a good map."

Ogden Museum of Southern Art   24 | 27 | 24 | M |
925 Camp St. (Magazine St.), 504-539-9600;
www.ogdenmuseum.org
"Southern arts and crafts" that go beyond "the usual suspects" win raves for the "newest museum in the city" – a "marvelous" edifice that's "one of the few great modern buildings" in the Warehouse District; its "impressive" per-

manent collection and special exhibits, from glass to pottery to photography, "form a clear picture [without] overwhelming", and it's a real treat to swing by "after hours on Thursday night" and have a glass of wine while "local musicians" play.

Old Ursuline Convent   – | – | – | I
1112 Chartres St. (Ursuline St.), 504-529-3040
This "lovely" landmark, "one of the oldest buildings in the Mississippi Valley" and the embodiment of "history with a capital H", is slated to reopen in late January 2007; those who visited pre-Katrina say it offers a "cool lesson" about the early 1700s arrival of the French Ursuline nuns and the cross-cultural schools they founded, while its herb garden and courtyard serve as a "tranquil escape from the boisterous Quarter"; N.B. the Vatican Mosaic Exhibition is scheduled to run from reopening through June 1st.

Presbytere/Mardi Gras Museum   25 | 23 | 19 | I
751 Chartres St. (St. Anne St.), 504-568-6968; lsm.crt.state.la.us
Designed as a monastery to flank St. Louis Cathedral and match the Cabildo on the opposite side, this 1791 cornerstone of Jackson Square now houses a "wonderful" museum providing an "excellent (and G-rated) look at Mardi Gras" in a permanent, costume-rich collection that "shows off Louisiana's unique culture" in a way that "kids love"; Carnival connoisseurs say it's "magnificent" and "not to be missed", particularly if you've never seen the real thing.

St. Louis Cathedral   26 | 25 | 19 | $0
615 Pere Antoine Alley (Chartres St.), 504-525-9585; www.stlouiscathedral.org
"One of the great cathedrals in a country that doesn't have many", this Jackson Square centerpiece – built in 1720 and still chiming – is a "historical must" for most; along with admiring the extraordinary stained-glass windows depicting the life of Louis IX and the glorious Renaissance-style painted ceiling, you can acquire amulets like a "medal with your patron saint" from the gift shop, though sinful types might do better to "view the beautiful church, then pray for what you did on Bourbon Street the night before."

St. Louis Cemetery No. 1   25 | 15 | 13 | I
420 Basin St. (bet. Conti & St. Louis Sts.), 504-596-3050
Visiting one of the South's oldest cemeteries, whose dead are buried above ground inside "beautiful old statuary", is a "one-of-a-kind experience found nowhere else in the USA"; its "decadent decay" is "disturbing", "ghostly" and "poetic", and "even the locals love to put their three Xs" on voodoo queen Marie Laveau's grave; just one caution:

this "city of the dead" is in a "sketchy neighborhood" bordering the French Quarter, so all advise taking an "inexpensive" guided tour instead of going alone.

Woldenberg Riverfront Park   24 | 19 | 15 | $0
Canal St. (Esplanade Ave.), 504-565-3033
"One of the coolest spots in town (literally)", this "lovely" "linear" "green space on the banks of the Mississippi River" is a fine place to "get a real look at Ol' Man River" and "watch the ships go by"; it's nothing fancy, but suited to simple French Quarter pleasures like "munching on a po' boy", "listening to the street musicians" and savoring "the only place with a breeze in the city."

LOCATIONS

NEW ORLEANS

Central City
Ashé Cultural Arts Ctr.

French Quarter
Audubon Aquarium
Beauregard-Keyes Hse.
Cabildo
French Market
Gallier House
Hermann-Grima House
Historic N.O. Collections
Jackson Square
Old Ursuline Convent
Presbytere/Mardi Gras Mus.
St. Louis Cathedral
St. Louis Cemetery No. 1
Woldenberg Riverfront Park

Garden District
Lafayette Cemetery No. 1

Mid-City
Longue Vue House/Gdns.
New Orleans Botanical Gdn.
New Orleans City Park
New Orleans Mus. of Art

Uptown
Audubon Park
Audubon Zoo

Warehouse District
Contemporary Arts Ctr.
Louisiana Children's Mus.
Memorial Hall/Confed. Mus.
Nat'l World War II Museum
Ogden Mus. of Southern Art

West Bank
Jean Lafitte Nat'l Historic Park

BEYOND NEW ORLEANS

Darrow
Houmas House Plantation

Vacherie
Oak Alley Plantation

TYPES

Arts/Performing Centers
Ashé Cultural Arts Ctr.
Contemporary Arts Ctr.

Cemeteries
Lafayette Cemetery No. 1
St. Louis Cemetery No. 1

Historical Houses
Beauregard-Keyes Hse.
Cabildo
Gallier House
Hermann-Grima House
Houmas House Plantation
Longue Vue House/Gdns.
Oak Alley Plantation
Presbytere/Mardi Gras Mus.

Museums
Cabildo
Historic N.O. Collections
Louisiana Children's Mus.

Memorial Hall/Confed. Mus.
Nat'l World War II Museum
New Orleans Mus. of Art
Ogden Mus. of Southern Art
Presbytere/Mardi Gras Mus.

Parks/Squares
Audubon Park
French Market
Jackson Square
Jean Lafitte Nat'l Historic Park
New Orleans Botanical Gdn.
New Orleans City Park
Woldenberg Riverfront Park

Religious Sites
Old Ursuline Convent
St. Louis Cathedral

Zoos/Animal Parks
Audubon Aquarium
Audubon Zoo

Ratings & Symbols

👫 = Children's programs ⛳ = Golf courses
✕ = Excellent restaurant Ⓢ = Notable spa facilities
⊕ = Historic interest ⛷ = Downhill skiing
🗁 = Kitchens ≈ = Swimming pools
🎀 = Allows pets 🎾 = Tennis
👀 = Views

Ratings are on a scale of **0** to **30**.

| R | Rooms | S | Service | D | Dining | F | Facilities |

▽ low response/less reliable

Cost ($) reflects the hotel's high-season asking price for a standard double room.

Top Overall*

27 Windsor Court
22 Omni Royal Orleans
Soniat House

20 Royal Sonesta
W New Orleans
JW Marriott

	R	S	D	F	$

Bourbon Orleans, A Wyndham Historic Hotel ⊕🎀≈

| ▽ 22 | 19 | 18 | 19 | $349 |

717 Orleans St.; 504-523-2222; fax 504-571-4666; www.wyndham.com; 177 rooms, 41 suites

The "two-story suites with balconies are unbeatable" at this Wyndham "oasis in the frenzy", housed in an 1817 French Quarter building by the river; a pre-Katrina renovation "significantly improved the look and quality of the rooms", and though "food service is limited", it's close to "great restaurants and nightlife."

Hilton Riverside 👫👀🎾

| 20 | 19 | 18 | 22 | $300 |

2 Poydras St.; 504-561-0500; fax 504-568-1721; www.hilton.com; 1544 rooms, 72 suites

Sure, it's a "typical big-city Hilton", but it's still "nice being on the river" at this CBD "convention site" "connected to the mall"; the "huge hotel" is "rebounding well", with restaurant and fitness center remodels; however, even before Katrina, service suffered under a staff that "couldn't have cared less", and given post-storm citywide labor shortages, surveyors are "scared" to imagine "what it's like now."

---

* Based on overall average scores

InterContinental ♿︎≋   ▽ 20 | 20 | 19 | 20 | $425

444 St. Charles Ave.; 504-525-5566; fax 504-523-7310;
www.new-orleans.intercontinental.com; 458 rooms, 21 suites
A "great location to view the Mardi Gras parades" is in the
bleachers constructed for guests of this "friendly and convenient" Central Business District hotel along the krewes'
route on St. Charles Avenue "a few blocks from the French
Quarter"; "comfortable beds and nice amenities" along
with "friendly" service and "attractive public rooms"
"make this a haven for business travelers", but a few find
"there isn't a lot of soul to this place" otherwise.

International House ⚲♿︎Ⓢ   ▽ 20 | 23 | – | 19 | $249

221 Camp St.; 504-553-9550; fax 504-553-9560; 800-633-5770;
www.ihhotel.com; 116 rooms, 3 suites
"Like a mini-W but more quaint", this "hip", "West Coast"–
style boutique hotel in the Central Business District lures
"beautiful people" to its "very cool bar, Loa"; the rooms
are "nice" but "impossibly small", except for the pent-
house suites that boast river views, and the staff is "warm
and personal"; N.B. a new restaurant will soon take the
space where Lemon Grass was formerly located.

JW Marriott ♿︎≋   21 | 21 | 17 | 21 | $279

614 Canal St.; 504-525-6500; fax 504-525-8068; 800-228-9290;
www.marriott.com; 424 rooms, 7 suites
"Lovely public spaces" "so close to Bourbon Street" make
this the "perfect convention hotel", particularly if you "re-
quest a corner room for outstanding views and space";
you can get a steak and cocktails at Shula's here, but "it almost doesn't matter if they have any dining or fun facilities
within", given the proximity to the Quarter and a "cute hotel staff" that "goes out of its way with service."

Le Pavillon Hotel ♿︎≋   ▽ 23 | 25 | 20 | 23 | $309

833 Poydras St.; 504-581-3111; fax 504-620-4130; 800-535-9095;
www.lepavillon.com; 219 rooms, 7 suites
"Wonderfully New Orleans" from its "welcoming staff's"
"signature Southern hospitality" to its "charming, old-
style rooms" with "marvelous bathrooms" and the
"haunted feeling that permeates throughout", this
"grande-dame" wedding cake of a hotel in the Central
Business District is "aging" but still "amazing"; you "can't
miss the Sunday brunch" or the "make-your-own peanut
butter and jelly sandwiches", which are "perfect after
a night out."

Loews ⚼⚲♿︎Ⓢ≋   ▽ 25 | 24 | 23 | 22 | $249

300 Poydras St.; 504-595-3300; fax 504-595-3310; 800-235-6397;
www.loewshotels.com; 273 rooms, 12 suites
A "gorgeous lobby" leads to "large", "vibrant yet gracious"
rooms with "excellent baths" at this "very nice surprise" in
the Central Business District; across the street from the W

and "slightly outside", but just a "short walk" from, the French Quarter, it offers a "quiet", "more civilized" environment with "great people-watching" courtesy of the Brennans' Café Adelaide, which serves "playful takes on Creole cuisine" to a well-heeled mix of visitors and locals.

Maison de Ville & the Audubon Cottages ✕⊕₳≋ ▽ 22 | 22 | 24 | 17 | $259

727 Rue Toulouse; 504-561-5858; fax 504-528-9939; 800-634-1600; www.hotelmaisondeville.com; 14 rooms, 2 suites, 7 cottages
The former quarters of Tennessee Williams and James Audubon are about as "authentic" as you can get for N'Awlins, so book a stay at this "old-time" hotel and get a load of the local "'wow' factor"; if "staff shortages" have affected the level of service a bit, a renovation has spruced up the rooms in the 1800 mansion and nearby "nice" cottages, and the courtyard is as "beautiful" as ever.

Maison Dupuy ≋ ▽ 20 | 20 | 25 | 19 | $169

1001 Rue Toulouse; 504-586-8000; fax 504-525-5334; 800-535-9177; www.maisondupuy.com; 187 rooms, 12 suites, 1 cottage
This "lovely" "little" hotel is "a great place to crash after a full day" in the Vieux Carré, being "fairly close to" but "away from the noise of Bourbon Street"; service may be a little "slow" and the rooms "nothing special", but the "wonderful", pool-graced courtyard is popular "for wedding receptions", and Dominique's restaurant gets good ratings.

Monteleone, Hotel ⊕₩₳Ⓢ≋ 20 | 21 | 17 | 21 | $165

214 Rue Royale; 504-523-3341; fax 504-681-4491; 800-535-9595; www.hotelmonteleone.com; 545 rooms, 55 suites
You can get the spins even before you take your first sip at the "one-of-a-kind Carousel Bar" off the lobby of this allegedly haunted, "heart-of-the-Quarter" hotel, but it's a "great place to start the night" nevertheless; though recently renovated, the rooms remain "wildly different depending on where you are in the rabbit warren" (specialized suites bear the names of authors who once stayed here); the rooftop pool is consistently "great", however, and the "genteel service" can help you "enjoy your stay very much."

OMNI ROYAL ORLEANS ♯♯✕₳≋ 22 | 23 | 22 | 22 | $295

621 St. Louis St.; 504-529-5333; fax 504-529-7089; 800-843-6664; www.omniroyalorleans.com; 321 rooms, 25 suites
"From the chicory in the coffee to the French Quarter location, this is New Orleans" say visitors "staggering back from Bourbon Street" to their accommodations in this "beautiful hotel"; the Rib Room is an "excellent" place to dine, particularly on Friday afternoons amid the long-lunching locals, but for those who find "too small" rooms, the only real advantage here is the "rooftop pool and bar" with "great views."

Renaissance Arts Hotel 🏨➰ ▽ 23 | 23 | 24 | 23 | $349

700 Tchoupitoulas St.; 504-613-2330; fax 504-613-2331; 800-431-8634; www.renaissanceartshotel.com; 208 rooms, 9 suites

"An arty kind of place" amid the galleries of the Warehouse District, this Marriott-run property combines a "modern design" with a "laid-back style" that captures the "quaint, relaxed atmosphere of the best boutique" hotels, despite being much larger; there's a "cozy" bar and chef Chuck Subra prepares "scrumptious" fare in La Côte Brasserie.

Royal Sonesta 🏨➰ 20 | 20 | 20 | 21 | $349

300 Bourbon St.; 504-586-0300; fax 504-586-0335; 800-766-3782; www.royalsonestano.com; 478 rooms, 22 suites

Its "balcony quarters put you in the heart of the action" "overlooking Bourbon Street", but "if the partying is too much", this "lovely property's" "serene courtyard with pool and bar" can help you feel like the bead throwing is "a thousand miles away"; while "some rooms are top-notch and others need work", a "staff that labors tirelessly to fill the gaps left by the hurricane" is uniformly "impressive."

SONIAT HOUSE ⊕🏨 27 | 25 | 16 | 20 | $265

1133 Chartres St.; 504-522-0570; fax 504-522-7208; 800-544-8808; www.soniathouse.com; 23 rooms, 10 suites, 1 cottage

"The most beautifully appointed rooms in Louisiana" come courtesy of hoteliers who also own the antiques store adjacent to this "enchanting" Vieux Carré boutique, a member of Small Luxury Hotels of the World; "get a suite with a Jacuzzi" and "a balcony overlooking Chartres Street", "enjoy the lovely living-room honor bar", "do not pass on the breakfast biscuits and preserves" in the "courtyard garden", revel in the "wonderful, old-style service" and let yourself "live like a (wealthy) local."

W French Quarter ➰🏨➰ 22 | 21 | 19 | 19 | $469

316 Chartres St.; 504-581-1200; fax 504-523-2910; 877-946-8357; www.whotels.com; 96 rooms, 2 suites

For a crowd seeking to "go back and help the Louisiana economy" post-Katrina, this "small", "stylish" spot offers an "easy", "friendly" stay; the "rooms have that non-hotel 'it's really a bedroom' look", and the bathrooms' "Bliss products are a bonus", as is the "great food by Ralph Brennan" at Bacco; perhaps it's "not as cool as its sister" in the Central Business District, but its "incredible location" in the Quarter helps give it an "up-and-coming" status.

WINDSOR COURT HOTEL 🍴✕➰➰🏨➰ 27 | 28 | 27 | 26 | $450

300 Gravier St.; 504-523-6000; fax 504-596-4513; 800-262-2662; www.windsorcourthotel.com; 266 suites, 58 rooms

With their signature "sense of grace and style" "in spite of the devastation", the "impeccable" staff at "New Orleans' premier hotel" "makes you feel like a king", "providing exactly what you want" before you even know it; though some rooms might be a bit "worn", "luxurious" suites and other "elegant" facets lead guests to conclude that "this gem is still full of luster"; N.B. chef Michael Collins now dons the top toque at the highly rated New Orleans Grill.

W New Orleans 🏨🏊

| 23 | 21 | 18 | 20 | $459 |

333 Poydras St.; 504-525-9444; fax 504-581-7179; 877-946-8357; www.whotels.com; 400 rooms, 23 suites

"Strangely chic" for its Central Business District location "next to the historic but down-at-the-heels" Mothers Restaurant, this boutique-y "escape from the typical business mega-hotels" is a "modern", "interesting and fun" place to bed, or perch on a couch indoors or out and sip among the "hip"; some of the rooms are "nicer and larger than the typical W's", and the service is more "welcoming", but there are still those "edgy, small and dark" quarters as well.

Wyndham at Canal Place 🏨🏊

▽ | 21 | 19 | 20 | 20 | $129 |

100 Rue Iberville; 504-566-7006; fax 504-553-5133; 800-822-4200; www.wyndham.com; 398 rooms, 40 suites

The accommodations might be "nothing special", but their city and "river views are spectacular" at this Central Business District chainster "a stone's throw from Harrah's casino", the aquarium and the mighty Mississippi; but critics complain of the "inconvenient check-in", finding "much trouble" to "transfer from the street-to-lobby elevator to another elevator" to get to the rooms.

LOCATIONS

CBD (Central Business District)
InterContinental
International House
Le Pavillon
Loews
Windsor Court
W New Orleans
Wyndham/Canal Place

French Quarter
Bourbon Orleans
Hilton Riverside

JW Marriott
Maison de Ville
Maison Dupuy
Monteleone
Omni Royal Orleans
Royal Sonesta
Soniat House
W French Quarter

Warehouse District
Renaissance Arts

SPECIAL FEATURES & TYPES

Bed & Breakfast
Maison de Ville

Boutique
International House
Maison de Ville
Maison Dupuy
W French Quarter

Casinos
Wyndham/Canal Place

Children Not Recommended
(Call to confirm policy)
Maison de Ville
Soniat House

City Views
InterContinental
JW Marriott
Loews
Monteleone
Renaissance Arts
Windsor Court

Convention
Hilton Riverside
InterContinental
JW Marriott
Wyndham/Canal Place

Cottages/Villas
Maison de Ville
Maison Dupuy
Soniat House

Offbeat/Funky
International House
Le Pavillon

Power Scenes
Windsor Court
W New Orleans

Romantic
Maison de Ville
Soniat House

Spa Facilities
International House
Loews
Monteleone

Spa Facilities: Hydrotherapy
Monteleone

Spa Facilities: Yoga
Hilton Riverside
Loews
Wyndham/Canal Place

Super Deluxe
Soniat House
Windsor Court

Trendy Places
International House
Renaissance Arts
W French Quarter
Windsor Court
W New Orleans

Water Views
International House
JW Marriott
Loews
Monteleone
Omni Royal Orleans
Windsor Court
W New Orleans
Wyndham/Canal Place

Wine Vintage Chart

This chart, based on our 0 to 30 scale, is designed to help you select wine. The ratings (by **Howard Stravitz**, a law professor at the University of South Carolina) reflect the vintage quality and the wine's readiness to drink. We exclude the 1987, 1991–1993 vintages because they are not that good. A dash indicates the wine is either past its peak or too young to rate.

	'86	'88	'89	'90	'94	'95	'96	'97	'98	'99	'00	'01	'02	'03	'04	'05
WHITES																
French:																
Alsace	–	–	26	26	25	24	24	23	26	24	26	27	25	22	24	25
Burgundy	25	–	23	22	–	28	27	24	23	26	25	24	27	23	25	26
Loire Valley	–	–	–	–	–	–	–	–	–	–	24	25	26	23	24	25
Champagne	25	24	26	29	–	26	27	24	23	24	24	22	26	–	–	–
Sauternes	28	29	25	28	–	21	23	25	23	24	24	28	25	26	21	26
German:	–	25	26	27	24	23	26	25	26	23	21	29	27	25	26	26
Austrian:																
Grüner Velt./Riesling	–	–	–	–	–	25	21	28	28	27	22	23	24	26	26	26
California:																
Chardonnay	–	–	–	–	–	–	–	–	–	24	23	26	26	27	28	29
Sauvignon Blanc	–	–	–	–	–	–	–	–	–	–	–	27	28	26	27	26
REDS																
French:																
Bordeaux	25	23	25	29	22	26	25	23	25	24	29	26	24	25	23	27
Burgundy	–	–	24	26	–	26	27	26	22	27	22	24	27	24	24	25
Rhône	–	26	28	28	24	26	22	24	27	26	27	26	–	25	24	–
Beaujolais	–	–	–	–	–	–	–	–	–	–	24	–	23	27	23	28
California:																
Cab./Merlot	–	–	–	28	29	27	25	28	23	26	22	27	26	25	24	24
Pinot Noir	–	–	–	–	–	–	–	24	23	24	23	27	28	26	23	–
Zinfandel	–	–	–	–	–	–	–	–	–	–	–	25	23	27	22	–
Oregon:																
Pinot Noir	–	–	–	–	–	–	–	–	–	–	–	26	27	24	25	–
Italian:																
Tuscany	–	–	–	25	22	24	20	29	24	27	24	26	20	–	–	–
Piedmont	–	–	27	27	–	23	26	27	26	25	28	27	20	–	–	–
Spanish:																
Rioja	–	–	–	–	26	26	24	25	22	25	24	27	20	24	25	–
Ribera del Duero/Priorat	–	–	–	–	26	26	27	25	24	25	24	27	20	24	26	–
Australian:																
Shiraz/Cab.	–	–	–	–	24	26	23	26	28	24	24	27	27	25	26	–

ON THE GO.
IN THE KNOW.

ZAGAT TO GO℠

Unlimited access
to Zagat dining &
travel content
in 65 major cities.

Search and browse
by ratings, cuisines,
special features
and Top Lists.

For BlackBerry,® Palm,®
Windows Mobile®
and mobile phones.

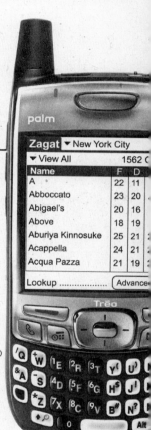

Get it now at **mobile.zagat.com**
or text* **ZAGAT** to **78247**